Growing Up with Roy

Memories of the '40s and '50s in Rural America

Galen Bernard Conrardy

Conrardy-story Books

Cover and interior design by *Conrardy-story Books*.

ISBN: 978-1-4116-8533-8

Forward

I've wanted to write a book for over thirty years. The initial concept for this book, *Growing Up with Roy*, began over seven years ago when I was teaching at Wray High School, Wray, Colorado. I enrolled in a writing course offered by Colorado State University in June 1993, at Wray High School. One of the writing assignments that I submitted was very similar to my episode on Blackie Graff in this book. A few weeks later when I took my son Mike to enroll at CSU in Fort Collins I began jotting down some possible episodes to write about – Red Ryder BB Gun, Little Moron Jokes, Where Do Babies Come From. By the time we returned home, I had a list of over twenty possible episodes to write about. Over the span of the next three years, I kept adding to my list, eventually coming up with over fifty episodes. I would add to and delete from this list in the ensuing years.

Finally, in the autumn of 1997 I began writing my first episode, entitled "Blackie Graff." When I would finish an episode or two, I would read them via telephone to Shaun who was stationed at Wright-Patterson Air Force Base in Dayton, Ohio. His reception to my writing and his encouragement kept me going. My daughter Sarah, also an excellent writer, has been very supportive of my writing, too.

In a few months, I had finished a dozen episodes while I was teaching at Sand Creek High School in Colorado Springs. In the spring of 1998, I decided to take a sabbatical from teaching and began working on my Master's Degree – finally! I sold tools and equipment for Mac Tools while I pursued my studies. So, between the papers I had to write for my classes and the computer work I had to do in the evenings for Mac Tools, my book was temporarily shelved. I may have managed to write an episode or two during that year.

I began teaching at a small country school, Edison, in the fall of 1999. My resolve to finish my book began anew. By late spring of 2000, I had finished a total of thirty-six episodes. I was fourteen shy of my target of fifty. I set a goal of having the rough draft of my book finished in time for Mom's eightieth birthday celebration in Stratton at the end of July. Unfortunately, circumstances prevented me from accomplishing this goal. So on July 31st I enacted a self-imposed deadline of writing two episodes a day (four to five hours of daily writing) for the next seven days. I didn't make it in seven days, but I did finish nine days later on August 8, 2000.

I've known people, including some students that I've had, who could sit down anywhere at anytime and write. Not me. One of two things must happen: either I have to be hit with a sudden inspiration, or I have to meet a deadline. Some of my best writings have occurred because of the latter.

The basic premise for this book was simply to write about some of the amusing situations that Roy and I got ourselves into – creative nonfiction, if you will. However, it has grown into an autobiography/biography, about growing up on a farm at Marienthal, Kansas, and covering the years 1948-1955. It is not only about growing up and learning as a youngster, but also about family, community, and Church during that time. I did invoke the writer's privilege of 'poetic license' where necessary in this book.

A word of caution to my mother Louise, my brothers Dale and Roy, and my baby sister Jan: please keep in mind that this book is solely based on my recollections and perceptions. If each of you were writing a book about the same period, then we would have four more versions – and rightly so. Also, if I have slighted or offended any of you in the least, then please accept my apology, that was not my intent. Yes, Roy is often the focal point of my writing, but then again, he was my sidekick during those years.

To Dad and Annie, I miss you and love you.

I want to thank my wife Judy for standing by me all these years. I love you, dear! To my favorite daughter Sarah, how can I ever thank you enough? You were not only my #1 fan, but also a gentle critic and awesome editor. And to Sarah's husband Kenneth, thanks for your support. To my talented son Shaun, whose successful writings have spurred me to get with the program, thanks! And to his wife Dawn, whose support and hugs have meant so much to me, thanks! Also, kudos for your editing expertise! To my sons Mike and Andy whose outstanding achievements in track and football have always been a source of great pride for me, and whose talents continue to amaze me, thanks! To their girlfriends, Kim and Rachel, welcome aboard! I love you all!

I hope that this book will be a source of enjoyment for all who choose to read it.

And Roy, I'll probably return your silver dollar, fifty-cent piece, quarter, dime, nickel, and penny – I owe you that!

--*Galen Conrardy*, 2000

"He ain't heavy, he's my brother…"
-- *B. J. Thomas*

for my brother Roy

1 Blackie Graff

"You boys better behave," Dad said. "Blackie's going to join us for supper tonight."

"Blackie!" my younger brother, Roy, and I blurted out at the same time. "He's gonna eat dinner with us?"

"Yep," Dad replied, "be in about fifteen minutes, so you'd better get washed up."

Roy and I were deathly afraid of Blackie Graff. He wasn't mean; he didn't hit us or anything like that. It's what he said he was going to do that was the problem. Mom thought we were just a couple of silly boys – at least that's what she told us. I remember she used to tell Dad that he was dashing like Errol Flynn. Roy and I figured he must be a pretty fast runner, but with his wavy, combed-back, black hair and mustache we really didn't think so. Little brother and I really dreaded when Dad had Blackie help him with the farm work, because this usually meant he would be invited to eat with us.

"Dinner's ready!" Mom yelled.

"Where are those two boys?" Dad asked. "Galen and Roy, get around the table now!" Dad warned.

"Do we hafta go in?" Roy pleaded, tugging at my shirtsleeve.

"Yeah," I replied, "it's better than getting Dad's strap."

"OK," Roy muttered. He grabbed my hand and we ran around

the table to the far end and scooted in around the horseshoe-shaped bench next to the wall.

"Whoa," Dad called out, "slow down! No running in the kitchen! Did you two wash your hands and faces?"

"Yeah, we did," I mumbled.

"Me too," Roy added.

"They look dirty to me, Dad," brother Dale was quick to add.

"March over to the sink right now!" Mom ordered, as she rose from her chair. Roy and I hurried to the kitchen sink. "Just as I suspected," Mom said, "you two didn't even rinse your hands in cold water!"

"Maybe I should come over there and give you a hand, Louise," Blackie laughed.

"Maybe I'll send them home with you after supper," Mom responded.

"I'm hungry," baby sister Jan cried out.

"Let's say grace," Mom said as we returned to the supper table. Mom, Dad, and Blackie did all the talking – weather and farm stuff – while we kids dove into the food. My favorite meal! Roast beef with mashed potatoes and gravy, homemade bread fresh from the oven, and sweet corn from the field. Lemon pie was the dessert; Dad's favorite. There was also broccoli. Roy and I tried shoving ours onto our sisters' plates, until Mom caught us.

I picked a piece of broccoli off my plate and tossed it on Roy's plate. As he picked it up to throw at me, I whispered in his ear, "Toss it on Anita's plate!"

"OK," he said, throwing it on her plate. She didn't even notice.

I nudged Roy. "Hey, let's dump all our stuff on her plate!"

"Yeah," he agreed, "then Mom'll make her clean her plate up!" It almost worked. Baby sister caught us in the act.

"Hey, Mom!" she yelled, "Galen and Roy are putting their food on Annie's plate!"

Before Mom could reply or take action, Blackie jumped to his feet. Reaching into his pocket, he pulled out a huge jackknife. "Come here Roy, I'm going to cut your ears off!" he said as he reached across the table. As quick as I could, I grabbed Roy's hand and we slid under the table, crawled between dangling legs, jumped to our feet, and dashed for the safety of our upstairs bedroom. I shoved Roy under the bed and scrunched in behind him, pushing him hard against the wall. We could hear footsteps at the bottom of the stairs. "I'm going to get you two!" Blackie yelled.

"I scared!" Roy whimpered as he clutched at my shirt.

"Me, too!" I hushed back at him. Suddenly I could feel wet at the small of my back. "Dang it, Roy," I blurted out as laughter filtered up the stairs from the kitchen below.

2 Afraid of Heights

"Your turn, Galen," cousin Billy said as he climbed up the ladder to the hayloft in their barn.

"He's a fraidy cat," Roy teased.

"I am not," I retorted.

"Then go ahead and jump," Billy demanded.

"Fraidy cat, fraidy cat," Roy chimed in.

"I would, but I hurt my foot," I said, demonstrating a pronounced limp.

We were visiting Uncle Anthony and Aunt Rose's farm, which was located two miles north of our farm, one summer afternoon when Billy decided we'd jump from the hayloft onto a pile of straw in their barn. The hayloft was approximately ten feet high and it was accessible by climbing a permanently attached wooden ladder in the middle of the barn. At one end of the barn, a huge pile of hay straw lay on the floor.

After leading us up to the hayloft, Billy took a running leap and landed on the straw pile below with a daring laugh. "Come on you two," he yelled.

Roy didn't hesitate. He went to the edge of the hayloft and launched himself into midair. "That was fun," he declared as he rolled off the hay pile.

Going up the ladder was bad enough, but as I inched my way

towards the edge of the hayloft I suddenly froze in my tracks. No way was I going over the edge!

"Well," Billy said, "we're waiting. Are you going to jump, or are you chicken?"

"Yeah, yellow chicken," Roy added.

"Hey, that's a good one, Roy! A big, yellow chicken!"

I was on the verge of tears. I had to save face. I turned, ran, and jumped over the edge of the hayloft, screaming wildly as I plummeted onto the hay below.

"Way to go!" Billy hollered down at me. I brushed the straw from my face and grinned up at him. The adrenaline rush tingled from head to toe as I made my way back up the ladder to the loft. The rush continued to wash over me several jumps later.

*****

When I was younger Dad had taken me for a medical checkup in Dodge City for a hernia condition. The doctor's office was located on the top floor of a five-story building. As we entered the building, Dad said, "Let's take the elevator up to the doctor's office instead of going up the stairs."

"What's an elevator?" I asked.

"Well, let's see," he pondered, "these sliding doors will open after I push this button here. Then we will step inside. The doors will close and we'll push another button and it'll carry us up to the doctor's office."

"How big is it?"

"Well, it's like getting into a big box."

"How does it get up to the doctor's office?"

"It's pulled up by a steel cord, like when you play with your yo-yo."

"You mean we'll be tumbling around inside of it?"

"No, we won't. You can hold onto my hand."

"What if the cord breaks and we fall? We'll get smashed!" I was beginning to tremble.

"No we won't. Are you afraid to get on the elevator, Galen?"

"Yes," I muttered, afraid to look up.

"Don't get upset, we can walk up the stairs."

Dad didn't get mad at me. I just didn't want to have anything to do with being yo-yoed up in a closed box called an elevator. I overheard Dad chuckling as he recounted the incident later that evening for Mom.

3 Outhouses

The infamous outhouse. It was a necessity on a farm in a rural community in the 1940's and 50's. In these days of modern plumbing, they are rare; except for the occasional appearance perched on top of homecoming bonfires.

When I was two years old, Mom and Dad moved from a farm east of Dodge City to a farm near Marienthal in western Kansas. With the help of Grandpa Klenke, who was a carpenter, they added a huge kitchen area to the old two-story frame house. Many other farm buildings such as a barn, chicken house, Quonset, and garage were added later. A new outhouse was constructed approximately one hundred yards east of the house. It was eight feet tall, five feet wide, and had two holes cut in the wooden bench, which stood three feet off the wooden floor. The smaller hole was for us kids, the larger hole was for the adults. Old catalogs like Sears and Roebuck, Montgomery Wards, or J.C. Penny's, were the toilet paper of choice. These catalogs also served as a constant reminder of Christmas and birthday wish lists.

With the ubiquity of outhouses back then, there was quite a variety of design. Some had a half moon or stars carved above the door. Some were painted in a particular color, or many colors. Ours was white, with a few vent holes located under the eaves of the apex of the roof. Some had two 'rooms'; one side for the ladies and one side for the men. Most outhouses had two latches on the doors; one on the outside and one on the inside. If the latch on the outside was hooked, then the outhouse was unoccupied. If it was unlatched, then it was in use. The story goes that this double latch idea came about because several people had been unexpectedly doused by pails of water while sitting on their thrones.

Outhouses were legendary in the annals of pranksters. They were graffiti-prone and susceptible to unsolicited paint jobs. They were often tipped over when someone was busy doing his duty. Pranksters struck most frequently during the Halloween season. On Halloween night many outhouses were relocated to Main Street, inspiring many sermons from the pulpit on Sunday morning. Dad's favorite recollection of Halloween when he was a boy was when he and some buddies moved an outhouse. It belonged to a grouchy old bachelor who lived in the small town of Wright. The old bachelor had refused to answer their many knocks on his front door when they were trick-or-treating for goodies. The boys finally gave up their futile attempts to get his attention and decided that a trick was in order. After an excited, whispered discussion on how to trick the old gent, they attempted to move his outhouse. The outhouse would hardly budge, so they had to run around town and round up some more trick-or-treaters to help them. Finally, they were able to lift the outhouse. They set it down right behind the exposed hole. Shortly after they retreated and hid behind some bushes, the old bachelor came out to use the outhouse and promptly fell into the hole. He eventually managed to pull himself out. As he fumbled his way back to the house, his wild expletives drowned out the muffled laughter of Dad and his buddies.

There's nothing more miserable than sitting in an outhouse in sub-zero temperatures. Those tiny shacks were not air-conditioned, much less heated. Doing your business in the outhouse during the winter months reached record-breaking speeds. However, as our grandparents were quick to point out, it beat sitting unprotected in the bushes.

My first recollection of the outhouse was around the time our new one had been built. Brother Dale had been instructed to give Roy and me a tour of the new facility and to show us the proper way to use it. This thirty-second tour ended with big brother giving his two younger brothers a demonstration in order to frighten us. "Hey, watch this!" he said as he climbed up on the seat.

"Watcha gonna do?" Roy inquired.

"I'm going to disappear down into the hole," he grinned. "Here, hold my cap, Galen."

"What for?" I asked worriedly.

"Cause I don't want to lose it in this shit hole."

"Please don't!" I cried out.

"Yeah, don't do it!" Roy added. Roy and I had both peeked down through the holes, and it sure looked like a long way down to the bottom.

Dale slowly lowered himself down through the hole that was designated for the adults. Roy and I protested with all of our might by screaming and yelling for help. Dale was now holding onto the rim of the hole with his hands taunting us with threats that he was going to let go. He finally managed to pull himself up and out through the hole only after we had threatened to go get Mom from the kitchen.

Constipation was a big problem for me during those days. I was willing to suffer agonizing tummy aches to avoid sitting in that outhouse. Memories of my brother Dale dangling from the hole haunted me for months. Of course, Mother's enemas eventually cured me of my phobia.

4 First Communion and First Confession

The most significant events in the spiritual life of a six-year-old Catholic are First Confession and First Communion. I was afraid of First Confession, but very excited about First Communion. First Confession meant that we had to tell our sins to a priest in the church confessional. And you couldn't receive First Communion unless you had already gone to confession.

Our religious education during first grade focused on these two important events. The nuns instructed us on the step-by-step procedures of the Mass – which we were vaguely familiar with since we attended church regularly with our families. We had to memorize several prayers, such as the Our Father, the Hail Mary, the Apostles Creed, and the Act of Contrition. Memorization came easy for me, so this was the easy part. However, I still had to recite these prayers for Mother at least once a week leading up to the big day. Of course, my tag-a-long little brother, Roy, always wanted to join in. "My turn! My turn!" he kept interjecting.

"Make him get out of here!" I pleaded with Mom.

"Now Galen, be patient," Mom replied. "Roy just wants to learn his prayers, too."

"No he doesn't! He's just being a smart aleck. It's not his First Communion, it's mine!"

"Yes, I know it is. Roy, if you go out in the kitchen and play, you can have a cookie."

"OK!" he shouted as he ran through the living room towards the kitchen.

"Not fair!" I protested. "I want a cookie!"

"Oh hush! You can have a cookie as soon as you finish reciting your prayers for me."

I think Mom was getting a little frustrated with my younger brother and me. Every time I had to recite my prayers for her it was like a broken record, at least that's what I overheard her tell Dad once. It was unusual, but on this particular evening, Mom was prepared to do the unthinkable, bribe me! "I'll tell you what, Galen," she mused, "why don't you start teaching Roy these prayers? You know them by heart already."

"No way! It's my First Communion!"

"I know it is Galen, but if you'll start teaching Roy these prayers, I'll pay you."

"Really?" I said, somewhat shocked by what I had just heard. "How long do I have to do it?"

"Just for a couple of weeks, until your First Communion is over. I'll have you practice with Roy after you recite your prayers for me, OK?"

"How much money you going to pay me?"

"I'll give you fifty cents, a quarter now, and then a quarter after your First Communion. How does that sound?"

"Wow! Fifty cents! Are you sure?"

"Yes," she replied, fatigue etched on her face.

After I finished reciting my prayers Mom gave me a quarter. Now I had to start fulfilling my end of the bargain. I went into the kitchen and found Roy hard at play with his toys on the floor. I asked him if he wanted to learn some of my prayers. "Really?" he asked in astonishment.

"Really," I said.

"OK!"

"Let's go upstairs to our bedroom and I'll teach you." I grabbed Roy by the hand and jerked him off the floor. When we reached our room, I closed the door and sat him down on the bed. "How much you going to pay me," I demanded.

"What do I have to pay you for?"

"For teaching you my prayers."

"How much do I have to pay you?"

"How much you got?"

"I don't know for sure."

"Well, find out!"

"OK, but you have to leave the room first."

"OK, but it better not take you too long." I stepped out of our bedroom and closed the door. I could hear Roy going through his dresser drawers. Finally he called me back into the bedroom.

"I only got three pennies," he said as he unfolded his hand.

"Are you sure?"

"Yep."

"OK, let's get started with the Our Father," I said as I snatched the pennies from his hand.

"Our Father, who Art…Isn't that a guy's name?…in heaven. How old be your name." This was going to be a long session.

The Big Week finally arrived! It seemed like it took forever, but it was here. We had to rehearse every day after school in church with the nuns. There were eight of us in my First Communion class, four boys and four girls. We had to march two by two from the rear of the church to the front pews by the altar. The boys sat on the left side, the girls on the right side. The crowning moment, of course, was when we could make our First Holy Communion in front of family and friends. At the designated time, Sister would rise from the pew behind us and beckon us to exit our pews and begin our procession to the top of the altar steps where Father would be waiting to give us the communion wafer. We were instructed on how to stick out our tongues in order to receive the host. And we were told not to let the host touch our teeth, we were to swallow it whole.

After school on Thursday, we were marched from our little one-room schoolhouse to church to practice for our First Confession, which was taking place the next day. We entered church and sat in the pews adjacent to the confessional. There were three stalls in the confessional; the priest occupied the middle one. When my turn came, Sister motioned for me to rise from the pew, genuflect, and approach the confessional door. I was instructed to open the door, kneel on the small kneeler which faced the priest's stall, close the door, and wait for the priest to acknowledge my presence. Once I was ready, Sister entered the priest's stall and played the roll of the confessor.

I dreaded telling my sins to someone else, especially a priest who was a representative of God. Our confessor was Father Eugene, a Capuchin priest, dressed in a brown robe with a rope tied around his mid-section. Father had smiling eyes, which was reassuring, and a long, mostly white, beard. Because we lined up according to height, I was the last one to make my First Confession. Sister had to hiss my name when my turn for confession arrived, because I had failed to catch her hand signal. A gentle shove in the back from Sister propelled me into the confessional as she held the door open.

I was shaking as I slowly dropped to my knees. I gripped the small ledge in front of the confessional window firmly in my hands and waited. Mumbled voices could be heard inside the confessional. I prayed for God to spare me this dreaded moment. Suddenly, the sliding panel door in front of my face opened, and a light filtered through the mesh screen. "Yes, my son?" I heard Father Eugene inquire.

"Bless me Father, for I have sinned," I stammered.

"How long has it been since your last confession?"

"This is my first confession, Father."

"Then proceed my son."

"Uh, I, uh, said three naughty words, told one lie, disobeyed my parents twice, and I didn't do my homework once." (Sister had instructed us to concentrate on the sins that we had committed that week. She said our parents had probably handled our punishments for wrongdoing before that.)

"Anything else, my son?" I was beginning to think that a good whipping would be better than the situation I was in right now. The good Sisters had hammered into us the hell and damnation involved with telling mortal sins. We weren't sure what constituted a mortal sin and what didn't, but we sure didn't want to be damned forever!

"Well, uh, I guess so. I traded two nickels for my younger brother's fifty cent piece," I whispered. I thought I heard a chuckle. There seemed to be a long pause. Finally, I could hear Father clear his voice.

"Well, my son, you should obey your parents, do your homework, and tell the truth. Remember, Jesus is watching you. For your penance, say one Our Father, one Hail Mary, one Glory Be, and trade fairly with your little brother. You may now say the Act of Contrition." While I was saying the Act of Contrition, I thought I could hear chuckles again.

Grandpa and Grandma Klenke arrived from Spearville on Saturday to help celebrate my First Communion on Sunday. I was excited because I knew they had brought me a present. Roy wasn't too pleased, however, because I reminded him several times that this was going to be MY day. I always wondered about Grandma Klenke. Every time they came for a visit, or we visited them, her first comments were always, "My, I can't believe how time flies," and "My, how big you children are getting!"

Sunday arrived! Mom fussed and fumed as she helped me dress for the big occasion. She helped me button my long-sleeved white shirt, tie my tie, get into my new suit, and tie my new shoes. After she checked my hands, face, and ears for cleanliness again, she carefully combed my hair and cowlick into place. Dad announced that it was time to go to church, so we hurried out to the car. I got the honored position that day, sitting in the front seat between Mom and Dad! We arrived on time for church and I had to stay in back with my classmates so that we could march to the front after everyone else had been seated. We proceeded down the aisle as the congregation sang the opening song. We held our First Communion candles in our left hands and our First Communion missals and rosaries in our right hands.

Most of the Mass was recited in Latin. Our new prayer books, complete with pictures, helped make sense of the Mass. Finally, after much fidgeting around in our new suits and the girls in their white, wedding-like dresses and veils, it was our time for glory! At the signal given by Sister, we rose in unison and marched slowly in pairs up the steps to the altar to receive our First Holy Communion. As the first boy and girl reached the base of the altar at the top of the steps, the rest of us paused as they received the host from Father Eugene on their tongues. After they received communion they turned to the side and descended the steps, the next two First Communicants would then ascend the steps to receive their communion. When our turn came, mine and Joyce Droste's, Sister nodded for us to begin our ascent up the four steps to the altar. As I climbed the third step, my new shoe slipped and I fell down in a heap at Sister's feet at the bottom of the steps. I could hear the oohs and aahs of concern as Sister helped me to my feet. My face turned beet red as I glanced at my family. Mom and Dad's faces were expressionless, Grandma looked shocked, and Grandpa appeared to have a grin from ear to ear. I couldn't see my older brother or my two sisters, but I could hear Roy snickering.

I think my face was still bright red when Mass was over and we had exited from the church. I received many thumps on the back and hearty handshakes from grinning neighbors. "You were funny!" Roy added.

Mom and Grandma began making breakfast after we returned home and my brothers and sisters and I ran upstairs to our bedrooms to change clothes. Roy kept recounting to anyone who would listen about my graceful fall down the steps at church in front of God and everyone else. Grandpa, upon noticing the increasing irritation on my face, beckoned me with a nod and a wink to follow him outside. I followed Grandpa out to his car. "Come here Galen, I got something for you." Grandpa opened the door and slid across the front seat and opened up the glove compartment. He reached in and withdrew a sack of licorice Nibs, my favorite! "Here," he said, "this is for you. I'm proud of you!" Those were the best Nibs I ever had!

5 One Too Many

The most popular place on the farm for us kids had to be Mom's kitchen. The heavenly aromas that drifted up from that special place could entice the most particular palate. Any time Mom baked, we knew about it. We were always eager to help out, because Mom usually rewarded with the pleasant task of licking the ladle spoon or cleaning out the remnants of the mixing bowl. Whenever chocolate or homemade ice cream was involved we were ecstatic! If we went grocery shopping with Mom, and we were good, she would often buy us a snack. Oreo and peanut butter cookies were my favorites. We could never open a sack of cookies until we got home from the grocery store. I loved it when Mom gave us an Oreo cookie to munch. It seemed like it was always Roy, Annie, Jan and I who shared these wonderful delights. I enjoyed savoring my Oreo cookie so much that I tried to be the last one finished.

"Hey, I bet I can beat you guys done," I challenged.

"Bet you can't neither," Roy said, accepting the challenge.

"I don't care," Annie said indifferently.

"Me, too," Jan chimed in.

"Last one done is a big fat cry baby," I admonished.

Roy picked up the taunt, "Cry baby, cry baby!"

"Am not," Jan cried.

"Am too," I pressured.

"Alright! We'll do it!" Annie said in disgust.

"Let's start with the middle," I suggested. The creamy middle that was sandwiched between the two chocolate halves was my favorite part. After we separated the two halves of the cookies everyone started licking furiously, except me. I was licking too, except I was licking the backside of the cookie half that was minus the creamy filling.

Roy would usually be the first one to yell out, "I'm done! I'm done! I won!" Annie would follow suit in a few seconds.

It always took baby sister a while to proclaim, "Me, too!"

"Ha, ha, boy are you slow!" Roy laughed as he held up his licked off cookie half.

The girls mimicked him by holding up their cookie halves and yelling, "Slow poke!"

Grinning from ear to ear I slowly revealed my cookie half with the creamy filling still intact. "Gotcha!" I announced with authority.

"Cheater, cheater, pumpkin eater," they cried out.

Sometimes a treat beyond our wildest imaginations appeared. One afternoon when Roy and I were playing baseball in the yard, Mom called to us from the front porch. "Hey, boys, come here."

"Do we hafta?" Roy replied as he got ready to swing the bat.

"Yes, right now, I have an errand for you to do."

"Oh, all right," I mumbled as I tossed my glove against the backstop. Roy did likewise and we headed for the house. "What do we hafta do?" I asked, as the screen door slammed shut behind Roy.

"I want you boys to take this cake out to the chickens and bring the cake pan back to me."

"OK," I said as I grabbed the cake pan from her. Roy and I took the cake and headed for the chicken house.

"What's wrong with that cake?" Roy asked me.

"I dunno, it looks like a good chocolate cake to me. Maybe a little flat though."

"Maybe it's poison."

"I don't think so, else we wouldn't be feeding it to the chickens."

"Can we taste some?"

"Hey, good idea!" We each tore out a piece from the cake pan. "Man, this is good!" I said while tearing out another piece.

"Yeah," Roy replied as he stuffed another piece into his mouth.

We were on our fourth or fifth piece of cake when we heard Mom calling again. "Where are you boys? I need my cake pan back, now!" We quickly cleaned the rest of the cake out for the chickens and ran back to the house with the cake pan. A short time later Mom beckoned us to the house again.

"Whatta ya want this time?" I asked in an irritated tone of voice.

"I want you to take this cake out to the chickens, too," Mom said as she handed me the cake pan. Mom's eyes looked red to me.

Roy and I delighted in stuffing our faces with the chocolate cake. We were over half- finished when Mom called out her warning for the cake pan again. Once again, we hastened with the empty pan back to the kitchen. Sure enough, less than an hour later we were summoned to the kitchen again. We didn't ask any questions as Mom, visibly shaken, handed us another chocolate cake to dispose of. This time we gorged ourselves with the whole cake. Mom never called for us again.

Later that evening when supper rolled around, Roy and I weren't feeling too well. "Why aren't you boys eating your supper?" Dad inquired.

"Yes," Mom added, "I thought that this was one of your favorite meals."

"I don't feel so good," I said while clutching at my stomach.

"Me neither," Roy cried out.

"Let me get the Pepto Bismol," Mom said as she got up from the table. I hated that pink stuff. It tasted like chalk. We choked down the Pepto and then Mom took us upstairs and tucked us in bed.

“I wonder if it was something they ate at noon that gave them an upset stomach,” Mom said as she returned to the kitchen table.

Years later, Dad would tease Mom about being the city girl who couldn’t bake a cake.

6 Jackass

It was funny how saying a word that you thought was so cool could get you in so much trouble, especially when we were repeating what an adult had uttered. Roy and I were quick to pick up on these gems when we heard them. Whatever was proclaimed in a loud voice by someone older than us always made an impression.

"Wash your filthy hands!"

"Come here!"

"Go to bed!"

"Get out of here!"

"Roy!"

"Galen!" We paid attention. It sounded god-like.

One time Roy and I watched in fascination as our hired man, Bill, worked on a wood project for Dad in the machine shed. We loved when he struck the nails with the hammer, often driving the nail in with one blow. It never worked that way when Roy and I would try it, though. The project was nearing completion when Bill missed the nail head and struck his thumb instead.

"Ouch! God damn it!" he yelled out in pain. He repeated this refrain several times while dancing around in a circle before us. He finally nursed his thumb by sticking it is his mouth. Roy and I stood there, awed by the dramatic performance that had unfolded before our eyes.

Later, when Roy and I were horsing around in the yard, he tripped and tumbled into me, knocking me backwards.

"God damn it!" I cursed at him. Unfortunately, Mom was hanging out the wash on the clothesline at the time. In a matter of seconds, she had me by the ear, nearly lifting me off the ground.

"You come with me young man! I'm going to wash your mouth out with soap!" she scolded.

"But Mom, I..."

"Don't you, 'but Mom' me, mister!"

"But Mom, Roy and I heard Bill say it!" I pleaded. "Didn't we Roy?" I begged. He was nowhere to be seen.

I hated the taste of Lava soap. Yuck! Phooey! Wait till I get a hold of Roy, I muttered to myself as I brushed back the tears. He was nowhere to be found. I hated to admit it, but it was sometimes more prudent to abandon each other's company at times like this. We finally wised up and changed the 'God damn it' expression to 'got dang it' – it saved our hides and mouths a few times.

Every once in a while we would hear a new word or phrase that would really grab our attention. One summer afternoon Mom had dropped Roy and me off at our neighbor's farm just north of us. An elderly couple that reminded us of our grandparents owned the farm. We were in luck on this particular day because their grandson, who was our age, was staying with them for a week. Bobby had a new double-holster gun set with two shiny, silver cap pistols. We quickly became friends. He let me share one of his cap pistols. I had to pry a nickel from Roy's fist first, though. Bobby and I were the cowboys; Roy was the renegade Indian. Roy was given a head start and I told him to hide among the farm buildings somewhere and we would try to capture him. A few minutes later Bobby and I headed out in bravado fashion to capture my elusive brother. Several minutes later frustration started to settle in. We turned over barrels, peeked behind wooden crates, crawled up on the haystack, to no avail. We finally started calling out to him.

"Come out with your hands up!" I ordered with authority. "Did you hear me!" I could feel something sharp in the middle of my back. Bobby dropped his cap pistol. He was stunned.

"Drop your guns," Roy demanded, "I got arrows sticking in your backs!"

"Jackass!" Bobby sputtered.

"What did you say?" I asked in amazement.

"Jackass! Jackass!" he proclaimed. Boy, did we ever like that sound of that!

"Jackass!" I uttered in reply.

"Jackass!" Roy said proudly.

A few days later Roy and I were deeply involved in one of our many adventures when our sisters rudely interrupted us.

"We wanta play too," they whined at us.

"Get outa here," Roy warned.

"Yeah, get outa here you jackasses!" I added.

"Jackass! Jackass!" Roy taunted in laughter, as they headed for the safety of the house.

Wham! The screen door slammed on the front porch entrance. Mom came storming out in her apron with a dishtowel in her hand. "Which one of you boys was calling the girls jackasses?" she demanded.

Brother Roy beat me to the punch. "Galen did," he squealed, "I heard him!"

"Ouch," I cried out as I felt the familiar tug at my ear. No wonder I was accused of having cauliflower ears.

"You march in the house right now, young man!" Mom said in a loud voice.

"Please, I'll be good!" I pleaded, "Roy said it too."

"I don't care," she said as she yanked me through the door and into the kitchen. Mom quickly turned on the faucet and grabbed the bar of soap. She vigorously jammed the bar into my mouth and tried rotating it around. My feeble protests were to no avail. "I don't ever want to hear that kind of language again. Do you hear me?"

"Yes," I cried out angrily. I went stomping out of the kitchen, down the short flight of stairs to the screen door, and flung it open. "Jackass," I said under my breath.

"I heard that!" Mom said as she yanked me by the ear again.

"No! No!" I protested as we headed for the kitchen sink again. I managed to stumble outside and I made my way around to the backside of the house sobbing uncontrollably as I went. I spit and I spit. I hated Lava soap. I stopped shaking and drew a deep breath. "Jackass!" I challenged as I looked to the sky. Something grabbed me by the arm and jerked me off my feet.

"I caught you again!" she said disgustedly.

The third time was the charm.

7 Slapped in Church

The most common punishments that Roy and I had to endure in grade school were staying in at recess, standing in the corner, or getting a swat from Sister's ruler across the knuckles of our hands. The girls in our classes rarely got caught breaking any of the rules. They usually just tattled on us and then sat quietly and grinned while we boys were administered our just desserts.

There were several catalysts for these disciplinary measures: talking when not called upon, teasing another classmate, throwing objects, passing notes, or not having your homework done. My cousin Billy had a knack for not getting caught, whereas I seemed to have a penchant for getting nabbed in the act.

Most of my problems seemed to occur when I was in the third grade. Third graders were the big shots because grades one through three were in a separate building from grades four through eight.

My first infraction involved the prettiest girl in our class, Yvonne Betlock. I was assigned to sit in the desk directly behind Yvonne's. One morning while Sister was instructing the second graders with their penmanship, we third graders were supposed to be working on our arithmetic problems. "Psst! Psst!" Cousin Billy was trying to get my attention.

"What?" I mouthed to him as I glanced in his direction. He pointed with his finger in front of my desk. It was obvious that he was zeroing in on Yvonne. I pointed at her and shrugged my shoulders. He then picked up his pencil and indicated a jabbing motion under his desk in front of him. I mocked his movements and he nodded his approval and then he pointed at Yvonne and grinned. Suddenly it dawned on me – he wanted me to poke Yvonne with my pencil! It was hard to turn down a dare, especially when it came from your cousin who was the leader of the class.

"Ouch!" Yvonne yelled as she jumped up from her desk.

"What's the matter, Yvonne?" Sister asked as she turned from the chalkboard.

"Galen poked me in the butt with his pencil!"

"Galen! Come up to my desk this instant!"

I eased up slowly from my desk. Billy and our classmate Bobby began pointing at me and snickering softly.

"Hurry up, Galen!" Sister demanded. I soon stood at attention in front of her desk. She pulled the middle drawer back and withdrew a wooden ruler. "Hold your hands out in front of you!"

I hesitated, but slowly raised my hands out in her direction. I then closed my eyes and braced for the worst. Wap! Wap! The sound reverberated from my knuckles. "Owie! Owie!" I cried out in pain.

"Don't let me catch you doing that again! Do you understand me?"

"Yes," I muttered under my breath.

"Now get back to your desk!"

My hands shook as I shuffled back to my desk. Yvonne averted her eyes as I neared her. "I hate you!" I hissed as I passed by.

"Galen's face is getting sunburned," Billy chuckled to Bobby as I sat down.

The first time I spent meditating in the corner of the classroom occurred a few weeks later, and this time Billy was also caught in the act. We were goofing around the outhouse when Sister surprised us. We shared opposite corners in front of the classroom for the next two hours.

Loss of our recess privileges was usually the most devastating punishment of all. Everyone looked forward to the freedom of playing and competing with each other during those breaks from class work. We were most often afflicted with this punishment after we began the fourth grade in the big two-room school. Some would say our hormones were beginning to play a part in our misfortunes. Even worse, in addition to the school punishments was the fact that it was doubled at home. Reinforcement at its best.

It was also during the third grade that I received a punishment that has left a scar on me to this day. This most embarrassing and shocking punishment happened near the end of Mass before the school day started. The girls sat in the pews on the left side of the center aisle by class, with the first grade seated in the front pew, followed by the second grade, then the third grade. The boys sat in the same order on the right side of the center aisle. The Sisters sat behind the students.

On this particular morning, Billy was sitting on my right side in the middle of the pew. Roy was sitting in the pew in front of us and a classmate of his, James Kerchen, was sitting at the far end of that pew. James acted a little odd at times and this morning he was really attention conscious. He kept making monkeyshines at Roy, Billy, and me. Most of us were well aware of the fact that church was not the place for this type of behavior.

As Father Eugene was giving the final blessing at the end of Mass, we could hear one of the nuns get up and leave the pew behind the students. Billy elbowed me and we grinned at each other because we knew that James was in serious trouble! We sat erect in our pew, staring straight ahead, in anticipation of James getting yanked from the pew by his ear. Instead, Sister Mary Agnes, who was the seventh and eighth grade teacher, took a giant step along the edge of our pew and slapped me soundly on the side of the face. I fell across Billy's lap in total shock. Billy and Bobby helped me out of church and tried to comfort me as they guided me to school. James followed closely behind us, chanting, "Galen got slapped! Galen got slapped!"

Sister Mary Katherine, our teacher, gave us a fifteen-minute lecture on behaving properly in church before class started. During the noon recess, Billy and Bobby cornered James behind the schoolhouse and administered retribution. A bloody nose was in evidence when classes resumed in the afternoon.

Mom and Dad, though sympathetic, stated that nuns sometimes make mistakes, too. Roy and I wondered if Father Eugene spanked the nuns when they were bad. We sure hoped so.

8 Mistaken Identity

Growing up on a farm taught us a lot about life, birth, death, and the opposite sex. Much of this knowledge we learned from working with animals on the farm. Of course, Roy and I also learned that mishandling them for the sake of sport was also educational in regards to our own personal well-being.

Dad always enjoyed and preferred raising cattle. He braved many a winter storm and endured many lonely nights nursing and caring for his livestock. We three boys often helped feed the cattle, but we could seldom participate in the other aspects of the operation. Mom wouldn't allow us to help with certain things regarding the care and maintenance of the cattle; she said we were too young and it was too dangerous. She was very adamant about this, especially when Dad and some of the neighbors were "working" the cattle.

The pregnant cows would always be early and start calving in late February instead of early spring. Dad always complained. During this period of time, usually two to three weeks, Dad spent many hours among the cow herd, observing, fretting, and caring for them. One of his biggest problems, and the one that caused the most concern, were the new cows – those giving birth for the first time. He often had to use a come-along to help deliver the calf. He would tie one of the ropes around the front bumper of the pickup and the other end around the hooves of the baby calf, then he slowly and carefully winched the two ropes together by ratcheting the lever-handled mechanism.

Early one evening during the calving season, Roy and I put on our jackets and took the table scraps out to feed the dog and the cats. On our way back to the house, Dad asked us if we would like to ride along with him to check the cattle. We were elated, anything to get out of doing the dishes! "Go tell your mother that you are going with me to check the cattle," Dad said as he headed for the pickup.

I ran into the kitchen with brother Roy hot on my heels. "Dad wants us to help him check the cattle," I panted, half out of breath.

"Me, too!" Roy chimed in.

"OK," Mother replied. "Please be careful."

"We will," we hollered as we ran back through the kitchen.

"Slow down," she warned.

We hurried outside and scrambled into the pickup. I had to shove Roy in first because I was going to sit by the window. His protests were to no avail because he was too small for a physical confrontation. "Take it easy," Dad laughed. It was a clear, brisk evening with an hour to go before sunset. We turned off the dirt road into the pasture where the cattle were grazing. Dad stopped in front of the pasture gate and asked me to open it. I unlatched the wooden gate and opened it into the pasture area. After Dad had driven through, I retraced my steps and closed the gate, making sure I secured the latch. I got back into the pickup and Dad drove slowly towards the grazing cattle. "I'm going to circle the cattle so we can get a count," Dad said. "I'll try not to spook them," he added. We always enjoyed helping Dad count the cattle. Whichever one of us got the closest to the count that Dad came up with earned bragging rights for the day. Roy won this time. His final tally was two closer to Dad's count than mine was. I convinced him later that evening to pay me a nickel for letting him win.

The most serious part of the cattle check was searching for cows who were about to deliver. We crept by many cows nursing their newborn calves. Dad carefully watched for any cow that might be lying on her side. We were cautioned to do the same. It appeared this cattle check would go without any interruptions until we neared the end of the herd. Off to Dad's left we spotted a cow lying on her side and kicking her legs. "This could be trouble," Dad said as he brought the pickup to an abrupt halt. "This is a first-timer," he added as he stepped out of the pickup. "You boys stay inside of the pickup."

"What's the matter?" Roy asked when Dad returned to the pickup after examining the cow.

"She's having difficulty calving," Dad replied, "so I'm going to help her." Dad backed the pickup behind the cow and then eased it forward to within a few feet of the rear of the cow. We could tell that she was struggling with the birthing process. Dad got out and proceeded to attach the come-along to the bumper of the pickup and to the hooves of the unborn calf that were protruding from the cow's behind. After the calf was born, Dad said he would need to go back to the farm and get some instruments to suture the cow with, whatever that meant. "Would you two boys mind staying with the cow and her calf until I return?" Dad asked. Roy and I looked quizzically at each other. "Don't worry," Dad added, the cow is too weak to get up now."

"OK," I said, reassured by the fact that the cow was helpless. Roy and I climbed out of the pickup to stand vigil over mother and calf while Dad headed back to the farm.

"It sure is a slimy looking thing," Roy pondered as he viewed the newborn calf.

"Yeah," I stated, "and Dad says the mother cow always licks them clean."

"Yuck," Roy said as he turned up his nose in disgust.

"Yuck is right," I agreed as I watched the calf trying to struggle to its feet. "Help me hold it down, Roy."

"OK. Look here, Galen!"

"What is it?" I asked, while holding on to the calf's head.

"I can see its peter!"

"So?"

"And it's got four tits!"

"You're kidding me!"

"No I'm not. Look for yourself!" I let go of the calf's head for a closer look. Sure enough, Roy was right! This baby calf had a peter and four tits!

"Boy, wait until we tell Dad!" I said excitedly.

"No, I saw it first!" Roy screamed.

"I tell you what," I said, "I'll trade you that big nickel I have for that little dime of yours when we get back to the house if you let me tell Dad first."

"OK," he said after a moment's reflection on the proposed deal.

It seemed like it took forever for Dad to return from the farm, I couldn't wait to tell him the astonishing news! Before Dad stopped the pickup we were pounding on his window. "Whoa," Dad said as he stepped out of the pickup. "What're you two boys in such a toot about?"

"You're not going to believe what we found," I said as Dad grabbed his instruments and headed for the cow.

"OK, what did you boys discover?" Dad asked.

"Look," I said as I shoved Roy out of the way.

"I guess I don't see what you're so excited about."

"Don't you see," I interjected, "there's its peter and here it has four tits! It's a boy and also a girl!" I thought that Dad was never going to stop laughing.

"It's definitely a boy calf all right," Dad replied, trying to control his snickering. Dad paused, trying to gather his thoughts. "It's like this," he mused, "you know those two round spots you have on your chest that have nipples on them? Well, boy calves have them too."

"Yeah," I responded, still not sure of the connection.

While Dad tended to the sick cow, Roy and I had a whispered conversation behind the pickup.

"I thought we got these things on our chests from the Indians," Roy said as he recalled a recent cowboy and Indian movie that we had seen. He had a good point there. I hadn't thought of that.

9 Will You Share Your Lunch with Me?

We attended grades one through three during the late 1940's in a little one-room schoolhouse heated by a coal-burning furnace during winter. Two of us boys alternated tending the coal furnace before and after school. Our tour of duty was a week at a time. This was a serious responsibility, one that we were proud to undertake. We were warned that carelessness could result in a catastrophic explosion. Of course, Dad's verbal warning of "Do it right!" was all we really needed.

About twenty-five of us were packed into this classroom. We sat in wooden desks facing the chalkboard at the front of the room. The coal furnace was visible in the left-hand corner next to the board. The American flag was also located in the front. After we arrived from attending Mass, we would hang our coats, caps, and scarves on the wooden pegs in the front hallway. A mad scramble was usually made for the desks, books were placed under the desktop, and paper and pencil were set out on top of the desk. We then stood proudly at attention and recited the Pledge of Allegiance. Sister would instruct us to take our seats. She usually began instruction with the first graders who were situated in the front of the classroom, while the second and third graders were instructed to check over the previous day's assignments.

When we made it to the third grade, we were Big Time, King of the Hill! We not only got to boss everyone around, we also got to sit in the back of the classroom! In addition, we were given privileged duties such as cleaning the chalkboard and erasers, sweeping, and dusting. Occasionally we were sent on errands to the 'Big' school for Sister. We coveted this opportunity on the one hand, but were apprehensive on the other. There were some awfully big guys up there! Of course, it was really cool when someone returned alive and unscathed from one of these missions. They would have an audience for the rest of the day – especially during recess.

Sister handled our "calls of nature" during class very efficiently. If we had to pee, we held up one finger. Two fingers held up indicated we had to take a dump. Three fingers meant we had to do both. Sometimes it took a while before Sister would recognize the urgency of our need. Once she did, she usually excused us to leave the building and go to the outhouses that were located one hundred feet due east of the schoolhouse. The boys' outhouse was located on the left side of the sidewalk; the girls' outhouse was on the right. Sears and Roebucks' catalogs were the reliable toilet paper. We figured that our parents took turns supplying them.

We always brought our lunches to school in our black lunch pails. We often had a hot lunch during winter. Our mothers filled our thermoses with hot soup, which were held in place in the lid of our lunch pails by a metal clip. I loved chicken noodle soup, hated tomato soup. Other than our morning and afternoon recesses, lunch was our favorite time of the day. Even though there was some "horse trading" going on, we were usually very stingy when it came to eating our lunches. Most of us were quite fond of the meals that our mothers packed for us. The only time I would part with any of my goodies was when my cousin Billy had some of Aunt Rose's homemade pastries in his lunch pail. Serious bartering would then ensue on a grand scale.

It was during one such session that younger brother Roy rudely interrupted me. "Hey, Galen, can I have some of your lunch?"

"What!? Are you crazy? Eat your own lunch, you moron!"

"But I forgot mine," he whined.

"What? How could you do that?"

"I think I left it in the car."

"Oh, that's just great! Well, you aren't going to get any of mine!" I declared.

"Please, purty please!" Roy begged.

"OK, but it's going to cost you a dime!" I demanded.

"I can't find it," he said, after carefully searching all the pockets on his bib overalls.

"That's too bad, uh, how's about that little pocket knife – do you have it on you?"

"I can't find it either," he lamented after a quick search of his pockets again.

"Well I guess you're just outa luck, then," I said firmly.

"I'm gonna tell Mom," he whimpered, as tears welled up in his eyes.

"See if I care, you big baby!" He turned and ran out of the classroom. Billy and I concluded our trade and began enjoying the fruits of our bargain. A few minutes later Roy returned hand in hand with Sister. Apparently, Roy had run to the Sisters' house, which was situated just a hundred yards north of the school, and tattled on me.

"What's this I hear about you not being willing to share your lunch with your younger brother," she scolded. Roy clutched her hand as he hid behind her.

"Well, it's my lunch," I replied. "He forgot his."

"There's no reason you can't share your lunch with him," she retorted.

"I ain't gonna share with him," I said defiantly, realizing that my classmates were staring at me. It was necessary that I save face in front of them.

"Fine," Sister stated in an air of exasperation. "Roy, you can come along and eat with us."

Later that evening after chores were finished and we had eaten our supper, Dad beckoned me to the punishment chair. I approached him reluctantly, puzzled as to what chore I had failed to do or what I could have possibly said to someone that was inappropriate. "What's this I hear about you not sharing your lunch with Roy today?"

"He didn't bring his," was all that I could manage to say.

"Well, I bet you remember to share the next time," he said as he lifted the rubber strap in the air. Dad was right, I remembered the next time.

The salt in the wound was that Roy enjoyed a full-course hot meal with the nuns that day.

10 Guy Lombardo Shirt

Our First Communion attire was store-bought. Other than that, most of our shirts and the girls' dresses were homemade. Grandma Conrardy was an excellent seamstress and we looked forward to her summer visits. She seemed to be in her blissful element when she was sewing, quilting, or cooking. She was a perfectionist in each area, even though she'd never admit to it. Mom actually did most of the sewing. However, because she was 'mom', I don't think we ever lavished her with the thank-you's and the hugs that we bestowed on Grandma Conrardy.

One of the most popular sources of material for our clothing was flour sacks. Mom would purchase her flour in twenty-five pound sacks from the local grocery store. These sacks were made out of cloth and had multi-colored prints on them, from floral designs to famous movie stars and cowboys. We always checked out the latest flour sack designs when we went grocery shopping with Mom.

My birthday was in April; Roy's was in May. The last present he opened during his birthday party was one from Grandpa and Grandma Conrardy. After he tore off the wrapping, he lifted the lid off the box and pulled out a neatly folded shirt. He gave a shriek of delight as he unfolded the shirt, revealing a portrait of his favorite cowboy, Roy Rogers. Almost everyone oohed and aahed over the shirt. I wasn't too impressed, especially after he kept flaunting the shirt in front of me and taunting me with, "Look what I got from Grandma! Now I'm Roy Rogers! Who are you going to be, Galen?"

"I'm Gene Autry," I said in disgust.

"Oh, yeah? Prove it! Where's your shirt?"

"I'll show you! You little moron!" And I shoved him back into his friends.

About that time, Mom entered the living room with the birthday cake and ice cream. "Galen! What do you think you are doing?" she warned. Before I could recover from the shock of being caught in the act, she set the birthday goodies down on the coffee table, grabbed me by the arm, and forcibly escorted me into the kitchen. "Are you trying to ruin Roy's birthday party, mister?"

"No, Mom," I replied as I tried to wriggle out of her firm grip.

"Well then, young man, perhaps you can explain to me why you were shoving your brother."

"He was teasing me," I pleaded. "It's no fair, I didn't get a shirt for my birthday!"

"That doesn't make any difference! Whose birthday is it?"

"It's… it's his, I guess."

"There's no guessing to it! You should be ashamed of yourself! Now go up to your room until I tell you that you can come down!"

I ran upstairs to the bedroom and slammed the door shut. I flopped down on the bed and hid my face in my hands. "It's not fair!" I sobbed. "It's not fair!"

That following Christmas Mom personally handed me my last Christmas present to open. I took the wrapping paper off and pulled out a shirt from the box with Guy Lombardo's likeness on it. It was a yellow shirt with Guy and his band done in a brown color. I was speechless! He was my favorite musician! I hurriedly put the shirt on over my pajama top and buttoned it up. After giving Mom a hug, I tapped Roy on the shoulder. He was playing with one of his toys. “Don’t even think about it,” Mom whispered in my ear.

11 Caught Smoking

Cigarette smoking used to be the thing to do – that is, if you were an adult. Dad and Mom both smoked when we kids were young. Our family doctor actually encouraged Mom to smoke because she had a nervous habit of chewing toothpicks. We were cautioned against smoking; in fact, we were told it wasn't good for us. Smoking was occasionally the topic of our conversation, especially when our cousins or neighbors were around. Emulating adults always found its way into our daily activities – and smoking cigarettes seemed very adult-like. Pall Mall, Camel, Phillip Morris, and Lucky Strikes were the most popular brands. A pack of cigarettes cost ten to fifteen cents. Billboards across America extolled the social virtues of smoking. Many of our favorite baseball heroes advertised smoking as the manly thing to do. Of course, if you wanted to portray the real gentleman look, you puffed on a pipe. The rugged, outdoorsman type rolled his own cigarettes. He would take a slip of white paper from a small packet, pour some tobacco from a pouch onto it, roll it between his fingertips, moisten one edge of the paper with his tongue, seal it, and it was ready to be lit. The real tough types smoked cigars or chewed chewing tobacco. The most popular kind of chewing tobacco was Red Man, a leafy tobacco with a picture of an Indian Chief on the package.

One Sunday evening our neighbors, who lived on a farm

southeast of us, came over for a visit. While our parents were engaged in a lively game of cards, we entertained our friends outside. We toured the farm premises to proudly point out new additions to the farm (animals and newly purchased farm machinery) before we got ready for serious game competitions. As we finished the grand tour of the farm, my buddy Duane spoke up. "Would you guys like to have a cigarette with me?"

"Are you kidding me?" I said in disbelief.

"We aren't supposed to do that," older brother Dale commented.

"Both of our parents smoke," Duane added.

"That's true," Dale confirmed, "but we aren't supposed to smoke."

"Yeah, but we will in a couple of years anyway. Isn't that right?" Duane pursued with his reasoning.

"Well, I guess it wouldn't hurt if we tried it," Dale said.

"Yeah, just one," I interjected, trying not to sound too excited.

"Me, too!" Roy yelled.

"Not you!" Dale and I blurted out in the same breath.

"I can too," he insisted.

"Sorry, you little moron," Duane quipped, "but I've only got three cigarettes. So that leaves you out. Scram!" Roy headed for the house, murmuring inaudibly as he ran.

"Let's go to the barn so no one will see us," Dale advised.

"Good idea," Duane said.

After throwing some rocks at a cat that we had chased up the cottonwood tree, we proceeded to the barn. We entered the door to what we called the milk room. This was the room where milk from the cows was processed for shipment to the grocery stores. Dale grabbed the string for the light switch and gave it a slight tug. I nervously waited for Duane to give me my cigarette. It was an incredible sight, with the word Camel imprinted towards one end of it. Talk about feeling grown-up!

"OK, put it between your lips, and I'll light it for you," Duane directed us.

"Do we suck or blow on it?" I wanted to know.

"You suck on it, you moron."

"Yeah, you moron," Dale echoed.

"Here," Duane said as he struck a match on the floor.

"Hey, what's going on here!" Dad proclaimed as he burst through the door.

"Yeah, what do you boys think you're doing?" Duane's dad, Fred, demanded.

Dale and Duane looked at each other with red faces, searching for an answer. "Uh, we just wanted to see what a cigarette looked like when you lit it with a match," I offered timidly.

"Sure you did," Dad said as he and Fred gathered up the cigarettes. "You boys best come up to the house and play," he added.

"Hell, you boys might have burned the barn down," Fred snorted. Dad laughed at that remark as he and Fred escorted us from the barn. Brother Roy was sitting innocently between Mom and Alda at the kitchen table when we entered the house.

*****

School officially let out the last week of April. A picnic was held on the last day of school to celebrate the occasion. In addition to the potluck picnic, several games and races were planned, with ribbons and candy prizes going to the winners. The first graders competed first, followed by the second graders and finally the third graders. While the chaos of the first grade competitions was underway, my cousin Billy, my good friend Bobby and I were plotting our own secret rendezvous under the railroad bridge just a few hundred yards to the south of the school grounds.

"Anybody know where we can get some cigarettes?" Billy asked as he tossed a rock at a nearby electric line pole.

"Nope," Bobby replied.

"How about you, Galen?"

"Nah, Mom always keeps them in her purse," I said. "Hey, wait a minute! I think maybe she put them in the glove box in the car."

"Really?" Billy inquired. "You think we could sneak some?"

"Sure!" I answered boastfully. "Let's go!" We headed out in a dead run for the car. Billy was the first one to reach the car. He was always first whenever we raced. Sometimes I wished he would trip or something so I could win just once. I hated the way he always bragged about it. He opened the passenger door for me and I scooted in on the seat and opened up the glove box. Lying there in the middle of the glove box was an open pack of Pall Mall cigarettes! We were in luck. The pack was pretty full, so we figured that my mother wouldn't miss three little cigarettes.

"Hey, whatcha doin'?" Roy said as he peered over the open window of the car.

"Dang it, Roy!" I yelled as I dropped the pack of cigarettes on the car seat. "Don't scare me like that!"

"How come you aren't with your buddies?" Bobby taunted.

"Because I saw you big guys come over here," he grinned. Roy idolized our cousin Billy, which didn't make me too happy because Billy sometimes paid more attention to Roy than to me.

"Do you still have that dime with you?" I asked as I fished for the nickel in my pocket.

"Why do you want to know?" he demanded.

"I'll trade you this big, shiny nickel for it if you'll leave us alone," I said while flipping the nickel in the air.

"I don't think so," he said after a moment's hesitation.

"I'll tell you what, Roy," Billy interjected, "I'll throw in a couple of pennies if you leave."

"I only have one dime," Roy muttered.

"I'm going to give you these two pennies for free," Billy laughed.

"Really?"

"Really. Here take them. They're free. They're yours for real."

"Thanks Billy. Here's the dime, Galen. Gimme that nickel." He stuffed his treasure in his pocket and hurried off towards the playground to show his friends his three new coins.

I took three cigarettes from the pack and put them in my shirt pocket. After carefully placing the pack of cigarettes back in the middle of the glove box, we shut the car door and meandered slowly along the edge of the school grounds so as not to draw attention to ourselves. We climbed the embankment to the railroad tracks and played follow-the-leader for a few minutes on the rails before we disappeared down the opposite side and headed for the bridge.

After we reached the safety of the bridge, I pulled the three cigarettes from my shirt pocket, handed one to Billy and Bobby, and kept one for myself. We strutted our stuff as we acted like big shots puffing on our cigarettes.

"Well, if we got 'em, we just as well smoke 'em," Billy informed us.

"But I forgot the matches," I said in an embarrassed tone.

"No problem," came the reply. "I've got my brother's lighter." Billy lit his cigarette first and then ours. We had a good time, puffing away on our cigarettes, blowing smoke at each other, coughing and spitting. Billy was most impressive. He blew a smoke ring that we could almost stick our hands through. Billy's older brothers were obviously good teachers. When we were done, we stomped out our cigarette butts and headed back for the fun and games. It was nearly time for the third grade competitions to begin.

After a great day of food and games it was time to head for home and get the chores done before supper. As we headed down the road Mom turned to me and asked me if I had been smoking with my friends. "Who, me?" I blurted out, as I gave Roy a dirty glance in the back seat.

"Yes. You!"

"Not me," I protested as my face started to turn red, "I was with Billy and Bobby all day."

"Don't lie to me, young man!"

"I'm not Mom, honest," I said feebly.

"I counted the cigarettes before I got out of the car this morning," she said, "and there were eighteen of them in the pack. Now there are only fifteen left."

I froze to the seat. No doubt about it, I was dead for sure.

12 Scrambled Eggs

Most farmsteads were self-sufficient in the 1940's and 50's. Farm families raised their own meat (beef, ham, bacon, and lamb), grew their own vegetables (most everyone had large gardens), and milked their own cows (for milk to drink, and to make cream and butter). They also raised chickens, not only for eating, but also for their eggs. Many farms, as ours did, raised or grew extra meat, milk, produce, and eggs to sell or barter with at the local grocery store in town.

One of the first outdoor tasks assigned to us when we were growing up on the farm was to gather eggs in the middle of the afternoon. I was the pro, having done this task for over a year. Roy was now my apprentice as he had come of age, being five years old. I had been an apprentice to my older brother Dale, who now preferred being Dad's shadow.

The gathering of the eggs ritual began at approximately 3 p.m. every afternoon. Roy and I begrudgingly began this assigned task after Mom's warnings began to sound like menacing threats. We would go down into the cool basement, pull the light cord on and search for our egg pails. We each grabbed two wire-mesh pails, one in each hand, and slowly make our way up the stone stairs and outside. The two-minute walk to the chicken house, which was south of the house, usually took Roy and I about thirty minutes to cover. A dog, cat, or chicken always seemed to be crossing our path. Dropped pails and a barrage of rocks typically greeted this interference. "Good shot, Roy! You almost knocked him out!" I exclaimed.

"Yeah," Roy said, "shall I hit him again?"

"Go ahead – no you better not," I said. "The girls might be watching."

"OK, I'm gonna get the cat up in the tree," he said with great enthusiasm.

"We better go get the eggs," I said as I headed back for the egg pails.

Before we entered the chicken house, we placed some loose straw, which was located near the entrance in bales, in the bottom of the egg pails to cushion the eggs from breaking. Then we entered the chicken house, flipped on the light switch, and began the task of gathering the eggs. We set the eggs that we found on the hens' nests carefully in the pails. If the laying hen was still on her nest, we grabbed her by her tail feathers and flung her across the coop. We really got a kick out of watching them and listening to their squawking! Sometimes, though, they would turn nasty and chase us.

We had a couple hundred laying hens at the time, which called for several egg-gathering trips. Each egg pail would hold twenty eggs, and we each carried two pails. When we finished gathering eggs we helped Mom wipe the eggs clean and place them in egg cartons, if we had to.

After we had filled our pails the second time and had exited the building, Roy noticed some meadowlarks sitting on top of the tin-roofed garage which sat just northeast of the chicken coop. "Betcha can't get one of 'em," Roy dared.

"Oh, yeah," I retorted. "Watch this!"

Splash! The egg disintegrated into a gooey yellow-white glob on the tin roof just below the startled meadowlark, which took wing in a hurry. "Me, too!" Roy shouted, as he heaved an egg towards the garage. He did make the roof, barely.

"Here, let me show you how to do it!" I bragged. The contest was on. Big brother demonstrated for little brother. Little brother emulated big brother as best he could. It was so much fun! Before we knew it, we had tossed seventy or eighty eggs on the tin roof. It only took a matter of minutes for the rancid smell of the broken eggs to permeate the air. We tried heaving pails of water on the roof, but to no avail. The water splashed harmlessly halfway up the side of the building. We hid in the shelterbelt of the trees for as long we could.

A week later I could still see the red and blue striped tic-tac-toe marks on Roy's butt, I was afraid to ask what mine looked like.

13 Easter

It was a long haul from Christmas presents to Easter eggs and candy. The cold, dreary days of winter didn't help much either. To compound this bleak situation it was Lent – forty days of fasting and abstinence leading up to Easter Sunday.

Lent always started on a Wednesday – Ash Wednesday. Catholics attended this service in order to receive the symbolic ashes on their foreheads. During the ceremony, the priest pressed his right thumb into a small bowl of ashes (made by burning palms from the previous Palm Sunday) and made the sign of the cross on the forehead of each parishioner. He then proclaimed, "Remember man that thou art dust, and unto dust thou shalt return." This ritual was for everyone, from infants to grandparents. We were all present to receive the ashes.

"My cross is bigger than yours," I told Roy as we got into the backseat of the car.

"Is not!" he replied.

"Is too!"

"Is not!"

"Is too!"

"Hush you two," Mom scolded as we headed for home.

On the six-mile journey back to the farm, I nudged Roy in the side and pointed to my forehead and demonstrated with my hands the difference between his cross and mine. At first he tried to ignore me, then he mocked my every gesture.

"Mom! Galen and Roy are making monkeyshines at each other," Annie cried out.

"Just wait until we get home," Mom warned as she shook her finger at us. Roy and I did a stare-down the rest of the way home.

As we exited the car Mom grabbed Roy and me each by an arm and marched us into the kitchen and proceeded to wash and scrub the ashes from our foreheads. "There," she said, "now your sisters have the biggest crosses, because you don't have any!" Anita and Janice grinned as Roy and I skulked out of the kitchen.

Later that evening, while Roy and I were drying dishes following the evening meal we questioned Mom. "Mom, what did Father mean about turning into the dust stuff?" Roy asked.

"Well," Mom began, "God made Adam from clay, which is made up of dust. And when we die we will eventually return to dust. However, on the Last Day, God will raise up all the good people in their bodies and take them to heaven with Him. So, you'd better be good."

I had a classmate who had a different version of where the ashes used by the priest came from. He claimed that his first cousin, who lived back east, knew the real story behind the ashes. According to him, at the beginning of every Lenten Season each parish digs up one of their dead parishioners from the cemetery and then uses that dead person's ashes for the ceremony. Even though it made sense to Roy and me, we secretly preferred Sister's explanation at school that the ashes came from palm leaves.

One of the things that Catholics were to abstain from was eating meat on Fridays. We kids didn't mind this penance at all. We loved Mom's macaroni and cheese dinners. She also made a variety of great fish meals; catfish was her favorite.

During Lent we were also encouraged to abstain from candy. We were each given a jar with our names on it to save all the candy we received for being good, doing errands, or getting good grades in school. When Easter Sunday arrived, we could finally indulge! Even though our intentions were honorable, Roy and I would manage to raid our jars several times during Lent. These raids were usually preceded by 'I dare you's'. We always hated it when Mom handed our jars to us on Easter Sunday. Roy and I usually only had a few pieces in our jars, while Dale had a brimming jar full. And, he refused to share.

When Roy and I were old enough we got to fill the Easter baskets with wheat on the Saturday before Easter Sunday. In late March, the resurgent wheat crop looked like lush, green grass. Mom would give us each a paring knife to cut the wheat. We usually cut the wheat from the field Dad had planted just north of the house.

I had Annie's, Jan's, and my baskets to fill. Roy had his and Dale's. "Be sure and fill the baskets up to the top," I reminded Roy as we began clipping the wheat.

"How comes?" he replied. "There won't be any room for the Easter eggs and candy."

"But if you don't, the eggs might break and the chocolate candy will melt."

"OK," he finally said, with a bewildered look still lingering in his eyes. I was willing to part with a nickel, if necessary.

After we had finished filling the baskets with wheat we headed back to the house. I let Roy lead the way while I lagged behind. I discreetly scattered half of the wheat from my basket before we reached the door. We placed the baskets around a nice Easter display that Mom had arranged in the living room.

I was very excited when I went to bed that evening! I relished the thought of finding several Easter eggs and tons of candy overflowing my basket. And then I would lord it over my brothers and sisters who would only discover two or three eggs and maybe a half dozen pieces of candy in theirs.

"Time to get up and get ready for church!" Dad yelled up the stairs.

Easter! I jumped out of bed and ran down the stairs into the living room. Even though my Easter basket had plenty of goodies in it, it wasn't quite what I had expected. A quick glance at the other baskets revealed a striking similarity to mine. In a panic I counted my eggs and candy. I then proceeded to count the eggs and candy in my brothers and sisters' baskets. Everyone seemed to have the same amount.

About that time Mom walked in combing her hair. "Gotcha," she said, with a twinkle in her eyes, "now go and get ready for church."

14 The Broken Wing

"Wow! Look at what I got from Santa!" Roy exclaimed.

"What did you get?" I asked, as I cast a quick glance in his direction.

"I got a double holster with two cap pistols!" he said proudly as he strapped them on around his waist.

"What else did you get from Santa?"

"I gots a pocket watch, a stocking cap, and a big pocketknife! What did you get?"

"I got a stocking cap, too," I replied. It was light blue, my favorite color, and it had white snowflakes on it.

"Whatcha got in your hand?"

"I got that lariat rope that I wanted."

I started to demonstrate by making a loop and then twirling it around my head when Mom yelled out, "Not in this house you don't!"

I laid the lariat rope down and picked up my new bow and arrow set. "Look at this," I said. "Now when you want to be the Lone Ranger, I can be Tonto!"

"Yeah, let's do it tomorrow! OK?"

"OK, but remember I get to use your pocketknife."

"How comes?"

"Because I have to make the campfire and stuff."

"OK," he said hesitantly.

The next morning, after chores were finished and we had eaten a hearty breakfast, Roy strapped on his pistols, handed me his pocketknife and said, "Let's go Tonto!"

"Wait till I get my bow and arrows."

Roy shot four bad guys as we maneuvered our way around the shed to the haystack. We called a time-out from our adventure to practice shooting my new bow. It was great! The arrows penetrated deep into the bales of hay from a distance of several feet. I shot two arrows; Roy shot one. We then retrieved the arrows and tried again. Finally the Lone Ranger reminded me of our mission – get the bad guys!

We hid behind trees, crawled across open spaces, and closed in on the outlaw gang that was holed up in the barn. The Lone Ranger let 'em have it with both pistols blazing as we burst our way through the barn door. "I got two of 'em!" he yelled.

"Keep 'em pinned down, and I'll sneak around them," I whispered as I crawled through the open doorway into the milking room.

"OK," he said with pistols aimed and ready.

I flipped out a blade on Roy's pocketknife as I maneuvered around the end of the stanchions. The Lone Ranger's pistols echoed throughout the barn as I slit the throat of one of the bad guys. I barely had time to duck, turn, and jab the blade of the knife into the gut of another member of the gang. The Lone Ranger gunned down the last bad guy as he was ready to lower the boom on me. "Thanks, Lone Ranger!" I said as I wiped the blade on my pant leg.

"My guns and my knife I got from Santa did it, didn't they Tonto?"

"Yeah, they sure did Lone Ranger."

"Who we gonna shoot now, Tonto?"

"It's time to eat," I replied. "I'm going to get my bow and arrow from the milk room."

"What we gonna eat, Tonto?" There were some sparrows and meadowlarks flying around inside of the barn.

"Let's see if we can get a bird with my bow and arrows," I said. I strung the bow, fitted an arrow to the bowstring, and slowly drew it back. I spotted two sparrows sitting on a rafter and I let the arrow fly. My aim was low and the arrow shattered against the concrete-blocked wall. "Dang it!" I wailed.

"You missed," the Lone Ranger interjected.

"I know, I broke a good arrow, but I'm going to shoot higher this time." I fitted another arrow, drew it back, and aimed a few feet above a sparrow that I had located on another rafter. The arrow was close enough to scare the startled bird into flight. The arrow bounced off several rafters before falling to the cement floor. At that same instant, a meadowlark spun towards the floor as it tried desperately to gain altitude with one wing.

"You got a bird," the Lone Ranger said excitedly as he rushed to the injured bird.

"Yeah, it was the one I was aiming at," I stated as I strutted behind him. The frightened bird backed up against the wall with its broken wing drooping on the floor.

"It's wing is hurt," Roy observed, as the Lone Ranger exited.

"Yeah," I said, suddenly feeling guilty, "I accidentally hit him."

"What are we gonna do?" Roy asked, panic creeping into his voice.

"Maybe we can heal it."

"How we gonna do that?"

"I dunno. Maybe we can put salve on it, or something."

"Yeah, but Mom might get mad."

"I know, we can sneak some out of the bathroom!"

"Hey, yeah! Let's do! But what are we going to do with the bird?"

"Let's lock it up in that little storage shed next to the outhouse." We slowly coaxed the bird with its broken wing into a corner near the stanchions. I reached down and cupped the meadowlark in my hands. "Ouch!" I yelled out in pain as it pecked at my hands. It almost escaped before I finally was able to cradle its head and neck between my thumb and forefinger.

When we got to the storage shed we found an old gunnysack and bunched it up and placed it in a corner. After we had enclosed the corner with some wooden crates so that the bird couldn't escape, I carefully sat the bird in the middle of the gunnysack. We latched the door and headed for the house. "Let's see if we can find some cookies to eat," I said as we entered the kitchen.

"Yeah, let's get some for our bird, too!" Roy enthused.

I gave little brother a stern look as I cautioned for silence with a finger pressed against my lips. A search of all the kitchen cabinets left us empty-handed. Apparently Mom had found a new place to hide her homemade cookies from us. "We'll look for the cookies later," I whispered. "You keep a lookout by the stairs and I'll get the stuff for the bird." I grabbed a jar of Vaseline and a roll of gauze from the medicine cabinet and quickly stuffed them into my overall pockets. "Let's get outta here," I said as I grabbed Roy's hand and dragged him through the living room.

"Where you boys goin'?" Annie inquired, butting into our business again.

"None of your darn business!" I retorted. We let the screen door bang shut behind us as we ran for the storage shed. Roy unlatched the door and I hurried to the corner, fearful that I would find our injured bird gone. With a sigh of relief I uttered, "He's still here!"

"How are you gonna put that stuff on him, Galen?"

"Well, I'm not exactly sure. Maybe you can hold him and I'll put the stuff on him."

"No way! I scared!"

"Big baby! I'll hold him and you do it!"

"I don't wanta do that neither!" he whined.

"Fine! I'll do it myself!" I unscrewed the lid on the Vaseline jar and scooped out a glob with my fingers. I gingerly picked up the bird with my right hand and I tried to carefully dab the Vaseline on the broken wing where the bone was protruding. In its weakened state the bird didn't offer much resistance. I sat the bird back down on the gunnysack and wiped my fingers on my pant leg. Once again, the bird offered little resistance as I mummified it with the roll of gauze. I was trying tenderly to tie a single knot with the gauze when Mom, with my two sisters trailing her, came bursting through the door.

"And just what do you two boys think you're doing?" Annie and Jan had smirks on their faces as they peered from behind her legs. "And what on earth are you doing with my Vaseline and gauze?" There was a prolonged period of silence. "Well, answer me!" she demanded. Roy had managed to disappear behind me.

"I scared," he whispered as he tugged on my back pockets.

"Well," I stammered, "I, uh, we were fixing up this meadowlark. It has a broken wing. We found it in the barn."

"Yeah, Galen sho—" A quick elbow in Roy's stomach saved me from any further explanations.

"Let me see," Mom exclaimed as she brushed by us. After a close examination of the bird all she could muster was, "Oh, poor thing! Next time ask if you need something, OK?" She reached down and picked up the Vaseline jar and the remaining roll of gauze. "Let's go girls," she said.

Roy and I monitored the bird very closely the rest of the afternoon. With Mom's permission, we brought out a small dish of water for it and we got a small can of grain from the Quonset. It never appeared to be hungry or thirsty.

After supper was over that evening Dad wanted to know if Roy and I needed to visit him at his chair in the corner. "Not today," Mom said, with an approving smile forming on her lips as she glanced at us.

The next morning we were saddened to discover that our bird had died from its injury. We even allowed our sisters to participate in the funeral preparations and burial.

15 Red Ryder BB Gun

The Red Ryder BB Gun. The barrel was black, the brown wood stock had Red Ryder's face stamped on it, it had lever action, and we had one!

"I think it's Christmas!" Roy exclaimed.

"Yeah, I can see light coming through the window," I whispered back excitedly.

"Let's sneak downstairs and look under the tree," Roy urged.

"OK," I replied, "but we don't want to wake Mom and Dad up!"

"Yeah, Dad might get his strap out!"

We shivered as our feet touched the cold hardwood floor of our upstairs bedroom that we shared with brother Dale. We slipped silently out of our bedroom and eased past our sisters' bedroom. Our hands slid along the railing as we tiptoed to the head of the stairs. I grabbed Roy's hand and we cautiously eased our way down the stairs. We avoided the creaky step as best we could and finally arrived at the bottom of the staircase. The glass-paned door to the living room cried for oil as we inched it open. We wormed our way through the slight opening and hurried to the tree in the corner of the room. The lights on the ceiling-tall tree alternated their Christmas greetings as we stood in awe at the mountain of gift-wrapped presents stuffed under its branches. It didn't take long to find our coveted prize! We could tell by the outline of the present that one of our Christmas wishes had come true! It was the only one we consented to share. Dale's name was on the present too, but Roy and I would claim ownership – most of the time.

"Let's play cowboys and Indians," Roy said. "I'll be Lone Ranger and you be Tonto."

"No way," I scoffed, "I'm Gene Autry." We strapped on our holsters with our trusty cap pistols and grabbed our stick horses and headed for the pasture. Roy always wanted to be the Lone Ranger because he loved shouting, 'Hi Yo, Silver, Away!' I liked the sound of my horse's name: Champion! I usually consented to let Roy carry our most important weapon, the Little Red Ryder BB gun. Of course, he had to pay for this privilege; a nickel or dime usually earned him the right to carry it. The actual shooting of the gun was on an equal basis.

Our cap pistols were great for noise, and we loved that, but the BB gun got results! Tin cans and pop bottles were our primary targets. However, the most excitement came from live targets, like birds, cows, pigs, dogs, and cats. If we were lucky we could occasionally hit a sparrow or a meadowlark, but our favorite target was one of the many cats that roamed our farmstead. They were the most fun because we could sneak up on them as they stalked their quarry. Just as one of the cats was ready to pounce on its prey we would shoot it with a BB. It would jump in the air, let out a loud meow, and make a beeline for safety! Roy and I would roll on the ground in fits of laughter!

It always seemed like our sisters were following us when Roy and I were trying to have fun. So we sometimes shot them in the butt with the BB gun to scare them away. Unfortunately, if we were caught, our punishment was to wait for Dad's strap when he got home in the evening.

One summer afternoon our neighbors who lived on a farm a mile north of us came to visit. Mrs. Yuse came down with her daughter Erma to spend the afternoon chatting with Mom. Annie and Jan were thrilled to give Erma, an eighth grader, a tour of our farm. Erma was a big girl – loved food – and our sisters kept her supplied with cookies and candies. Roy and I thought she was rather strange, so we followed them around for a while.

"This is really boring," I said, "let's go play or do something else."

"I got a good idea," Roy chipped in, "let's scare 'em!"

"Hey, let's do it! We could sneak ahead of them and jump out from behind a corner of the shed and hoot and holler."

"Nah," Roy interrupted, "let's throw something at them, like some corncobs."

"Or we could get some pails of water and throw it on them," I suggested.

"Ya know what?" Roy pondered, "Erma's got a big butt!"

"Yeah," I replied, getting the hint, "let's shoot her in the butt with the BB gun! Go get the gun and meet me behind the house."

"OK," he said as he darted for the shed.

Roy was gasping for air as he met me behind the house. We quickly checked for ammo and then stalked the girls as they headed for the garden. They were so busy talking they didn't see or hear us sneak up behind the car just a few yards away. "You can shoot her in the butt now," Roy whispered excitedly, "boy is it big!"

"Nah, you gave me that nickel this morning, it's your turn," I said.

"Really?" Roy asked

"Sure. Besides, you're a better shot than I am." I had also discovered that my spankings were less severe if Roy had his finger on the trigger when we were caught. "Are you ready?"

Roy squeezed the trigger. The BB gun really didn't make that much noise, kind of a muffled twang. We were disappointed; usually our targets made a noise when they were struck by the BB's. However, our two sisters knew what happened.

"We're telling! We're telling!" they both shouted in unison, as they headed for the house.

“Hey, come back,” Erma pleaded, “I didn’t feel a thing!”

Annie and Jan didn’t pay any attention to her; this was too good of an opportunity for them to pass up. They lived to tattle on Roy and me.

Two days later I could still see the tic-tac-toe marks on Roy’s behind, and feel them on mine.

16 Fourth of July

The Fourth of July was the "Big Bang" to us kids. Every summer the Conrardy and Wilkens families would take turns hosting this patriotic event. The Wilkens' were our close neighbors who lived three miles southeast of us on County Line Road. They had seven children, four boys and three girls. Louetta was the oldest, Dale's age, then came Duane who was the same age as me. Barbara and Sue matched up in the age range of Anita and Janice. Their three youngest boys were Fred, Jr., Garrett, and Cary Jay.

This was our year to host the barbecue and fireworks display. At the beginning of June Mom and Dad ordered a large assortment of fireworks from a mail-order catalog. A week before the Fourth, Roy and I started complaining that we weren't going to get any firecrackers on time. But they always arrived two or three days before the celebration. Our rural mail carrier hand-delivered the package to our doorstep. We had to wait until after supper to check and make sure all the contents were there. The important thing was that the box had finally arrived. Roy and I spent all afternoon arguing about who was going to get what. Mom locked the fireworks in their bedroom closet, so we didn't dare take a peek, even though we wanted to.

That evening Dad ripped open the huge box of fireworks. It was six feet long, two feet wide and six inches deep. Everything we ever dreamed of was there: Roman candles, cone-shaped volcanoes, sparklers, punks (to light the fireworks with), various sizes of firecrackers, spinners, black worms, and parachutists. If Roy and I had been on our best behavior that day, we could have pleaded our case for a couple packs of firecrackers, but not today.

Wheat harvest was over, the irrigated crops were growing, and Roy and I were fidgeting around waiting for the Wilkens' to show up. It was the afternoon of the Fourth and preparations were well under way for the barbecue. Dad had the homemade barbecue trough cleaned and filled with charcoal. The hamburger patties and hot dogs were ready. Mom was in the kitchen making potato salad and coleslaw. Dale helped by slicing tomatoes and onions from the garden. Annie and Jan were playing with their dolls and Roy and I were sneaking potato chips. "You two boys get out of the chips and go outside," Mom warned.

We went out to the road to see if they were coming. "Hey, I think I see some dust flying," I yelled.

"Me too," Roy said, pointing down the road.

"They're coming! They're coming!" we shouted in unison as we ran for the house.

"Whoa," Dad said. "They aren't here yet."

Sure enough, we were right. Fred drove into the yard in their big Mercury car. And before the car came to a complete stop, Duane had jumped out and we headed for the shelterbelt to pop some firecrackers. He always had firecrackers to shoot before we did. "Hey, not so fast there," Duane's dad hollered at us, "you've got to help carry the desserts in."

We rushed back to the trunk of the car and helped carry homemade apple, cherry, and rhubarb pies to the kitchen. Fred carried in the homemade ice cream. After grabbing a handful of chips we rushed back out to the shelterbelt to pop some firecrackers. "What kind you got?" I asked.

"Some Black Bears," Duane replied.

"Are they any good?" Roy queried.

"Watch this," he said. He pulled a Zippo lighter out of his pocket, lit the end of a firecracker and tossed it among a half dozen chickens that were nearby. BAM!! The chickens clucked madly as they scattered in all directions.

"Wow!" I exclaimed.

"Yeah!" Roy enthused.

"You boys better not be scaring the chickens," Dad hollered from the barbecue area.

"We're just popping cans," I volunteered.

"Well, don't do it near the chickens," he warned.

"OK," I said. "I know, let's find some anthills."

"Good idea," Duane said.

We took a small stick and poked a hole in the anthill. Duane let Roy and me take turns putting the firecracker in the hole and then he would light the end of the fuse with his lighter. We ran several feet away and then turned to watch the explosion. Sand, dirt, and ants mushroomed out with a dull thud. When we tired of blowing up anthills, we started on tin cans. Roy or I placed a firecracker under an empty tin can with the fuse sticking out from under the rim. Duane still had the honor of lighting the firecrackers. This was fun for a while because the cans would erupt with a metallic bang. Our next target was one of our elusive farm cats. We finally spotted one taking a nap under the shade of a tree. Before we snuck up behind the tree, Duane handed me a firecracker and said that I got to throw the first one at the cat. Boy was I excited! Roy protested until Duane consented to let him throw the next one. We arrived behind the tree without disturbing the cat. I held out the firecracker and Duane lit the end of it. "Hey you guys! It's time to eat!" Bang!

"Me-o-ow!" The cat raced up the trunk of the tree.

"Ouch!" I cried out in pain. "My side! My side hurts!"

"Let me see," Duane said, alarm and fear etched on his face. "It just tore a little hole in your shirt, and your side looks a little red is all."

"Yeah, but it still hurts."

"That's cause it's like a sting."

"Just like a bee sting," Roy added.

"No, it's like being hit hard with a stick," Duane said.

"Yeah, you big dummy! But it still stings pretty good."

"I know what," Duane interrupted, "let's sneak up to the house and I'll put some salve on it for you and then you can change shirts. OK?"

"OK," I muttered. It was my favorite Guy Lombardo shirt that Mom had made for me.

We sent Roy ahead to inform Mom that we needed to wash our hands and faces before we ate. Duane applied some lotion that we found in the medicine cabinet to my side. It was really soothing. I changed shirts and we joined our families for the outdoor picnic. The homemade ice cream was the best!

Dale and Louetta helped the adults clean up while the rest of us played hide-and-seek until it was dark enough to start the fireworks display. They also helped set up the fireworks. Dad and Fred lit off all the big stuff, while the girls and Duane's younger brothers chased around with sparklers. After viewing the brilliant aerial display of the giant fireworks, we had contests with our Roman candles to see who could shoot their cannonballs the highest. It was a great day; we hated to see our neighbors leave.

The next morning Roy and I were busy with one of our famous Dodgers/Red Sox games when Mom came rushing out to us waving a piece of clothing in her hand. "What's the meaning of this young man," she demanded as she shook the shirt in my face. It was my favorite Guy Lombardo shirt.

"I-I-I…"

"A firecracker blew up and did it," Roy said.

"A firecracker!" she thundered at me.

"It was an accident," I pleaded. "Wasn't it Roy?"

"No, the cat scared you," Roy offered.

"You march in the house right now young man," Mom said as she yanked me by the ear.

"But, but Mom!"

17 Gotcha!

When Roy and I got into trouble, we usually accepted our punishment. We didn't want to, but Dad was a giant. We always felt secure in his presence when it was stormy out or when we were scared of something. And we never ran away when he said, "Come here!" It was bad enough just hearing that command. Dad and Mom had a great system for dealing with us kids; usually Roy and me. Mom caught us when we got into trouble ninety-five percent of the time. Then, unless we were caught using cuss words, we were told to wait until Dad came in from doing farm work that evening. Mom handled a mean bar of soap and Dad swung a nasty rubber strap. Waiting for Dad to come in from doing his farm chores was pure hell. Roy and I would try playing games but our hearts just weren't in it.

"Boy, I hope it doesn't hurt like last time," I said.

"Me, too," Roy replied, "maybe Dad will forget this time."

"Mom will tell him, you dummy. She never forgets. Hey, wait a minute! I got an idea! Way to go Roy!"

"What'd I do?"

"Maybe we can get Mom to forget. Then she won't tell Dad."

"Think so? How we gonna do that?"

"Well, let's see. We could be nice to the girls. And, hey, better yet, we'll help Mom with her chores."

"Yeah, let's do it!" he piped in. We'd do anything to avoid the strap. We raced into the house to find Mom.

"Hey Mom, can Roy and I help you do any chores?"

"You two boys feeling all right?" she asked.

"We just thought we would help," I said, looking dejected.

"Well, OK, I guess. If you really want to."

"What do you want us to do?"

"Yeah, what do you want us to do?" Roy echoed.

"You can start by emptying all of the trash cans for me." We not only emptied the trash cans, we swept the kitchen floor, cleaned up our room, set the table for supper, and we also helped Mom do the supper dishes.

"Can we go play now?" I asked innocently as Roy and I folded our drying towels.

"Why of course you can," she said matter-of-factly, "that is, after you tell Dad what you two boys did this afternoon."

"Come here you two," Dad ordered as he lit up his favorite pipe, "what did you two do this time?"

"Galen made me shoot the window out in the chicken coop," Roy volunteered.

"No, I didn't!"

"Yes you did!" he cried out, "you bet me a nickel."

"It sounds to me like you're both guilty," he said as he got up to fetch his rubber strap that he kept on top of one of the cabinets. Dad returned to his chair and motioned for me to come over to him. "You're the oldest, Galen. You should know better. So you're going to be the first one to get the whipping." Dad grabbed me by the back of the shirt and pulled me face down over his legs. Wap! Wap! Wap! Currents of ouch surged throughout my body. "OK, Roy, it's your turn," Dad said as he lifted me from his lap.

As I staggered by Mom in the kitchen with my hands clutching my rear end, I blurted out, "See if we ever help you again," the tears streaming down my face.

One summer afternoon when Roy and I were playing our baseball game – he was the Dodgers, I was the Red Sox – Mom interrupted and told us it was time to hoe the vegetable garden. "Do we have to?" Roy whined.

"Yes you do," Mom said.

"But I don't want to," he continued.

"You'll do as I say young man, now!" Mom retorted as she headed back for the house.

"Come on Roy," I added. "We don't want her to tell Dad."

"But I hate hoeing," he said. "I'm going to get a drink of water first."

"OK, I'll get the hoes out of the shed and meet you in the garden." I went to the shed, found the hoes, and went to the garden. After I unlatched the gate, I set one hoe up against the mesh fence. Then I started hoeing between two rows of cabbage. That's when I heard a loud voice shouting from the house.

"Come back here Roy, right now!"

"I ain't going to," Roy managed to say as he ran down the sidewalk. Mom was hot on his heels. Her big apron was flapping and she was carrying a yardstick in one hand. I was amazed; I didn't know Mom could run so fast! Roy rounded the little shed and headed in the direction of the big cottonwood tree, Mom was right behind him. As Mom was chasing Roy by the big tree, she tripped on an exposed tree root and went down. She lay motionless on the ground. Roy kept running. I dropped my hoe and headed out of the garden to help Mom. About that time, she turned her head towards me and put a finger up to her lips to stop me. I caught the hint and returned to the garden. I picked up my hoe and pretended to be hoeing. I noticed that Roy had slowed down and was near the barn. He finally paused and looked around carefully, searching for some sign of Mom. Finally, he started edging back towards the tree. Soon he spotted Mom lying face down on the ground near the tree. He slowly circled around the tree, stopped and peered at Mom's motionless form.

"Mom?" he muttered hesitantly. No reply came from the lifeless body on the ground.

"Mom?" he called out more boldly this time. Still there was silence. Roy eased himself out from behind the trunk of the tree and tiptoed silently towards Mom. He walked around the side of her and approached her head. When he was a few feet away he bent over slightly and inquired, "Are you dead yet Mom?" A hand darted out and grabbed Roy by the ankle. The blood-curdling yell that followed sent shivers up my spine.

18 Nicknames

What's in a name? A rose by any other name would smell as sweet. This classic statement seems to hold a great deal of merit. It's amazing how many people look like the person their name implies or who grow into that person over a period of time.

We kids all knew that our middle names were in honor of a particular relative. Dale's middle name, Elmer, was in memory of Dad's younger brother who died at the age of sixteen from a ruptured appendix. My middle name, Bernard, was after my dad. Roy's middle name, Eugene, was in honor of Dad's youngest brother. He also had the only clearly defined first name – being named after Great Uncle Roy on Mom's side of the family. Anita had Mom's name, Louise, for her middle name and Janice's middle name was based on Aunt Rose's.

I asked Mom once how in the world she ever came up with the name of Galen. She said she had read it in a book and thought it was a cute name. With the exception of Roy, I never knew how she arrived at the other kids' first names.

Dale probably had the most trouble defending his name growing up as a youngster. After all, a couple of our most popular heroes at the time were Roy Rogers and Dale Evans. And I'm sure that Mom gave him the explanation he needed to explain the origin of his name.

I was the first one to acquire a nickname. Roy and I were riding with our hired man, Bill Lamb, in the pickup one afternoon. We were rounding up a couple of stray calves that had escaped under the wire fence that surrounded the pasture. Dad was pasturing the cattle on a field of winter wheat enclosed by an electric fence. A single round wire was attached to metal fence posts with an insulator clip on an insulator. A fence charger was strapped to a wooden corner post. Wires were attached from the terminals on the charger to a car or truck battery and to the fence wire itself. When the switch to the fence charger was flipped on, an electric current pulsated through the wire. If a cow touched this wire, it received an electric shock, thus causing it to stay within the confines of the fenced-in area.

Bill pulled up next to one of the fence posts and instructed me to get out of the pickup, unclip the wire from the insulator on the post, lift the wire off the insulator and lay it on the ground while he drove the pickup over it. Then I was to reattach the wire to the post. "OK, Galen, go ahead and do it," Bill said with a mischievous grin on his face.

I jumped out of the pickup and did as I was told. I thought I could hear Bill and Roy snickering as I grabbed the wire and laid it on the ground. Bill had a puzzled look on his face as he crossed the wire with the pickup. "Now I know why those calves got out," Bill said as he approached me from behind. I had just finished reattaching the wire to the insulator on the post.

"What?" I answered.

"Those calves got out because there's a short in the wire someplace. There's no juice going through it."

"Yeah, I bet that's it," I replied.

"Yikes! That hurts! Dammit!" he yelled as he jerked his hand free from the wire. "How did you do that?" he said shaking his hand.

"How did I do what?"

"Didn't you get shocked when you grabbed a hold of the wire?"

"No."

"You're kidding me! Grab a hold of it again."

"OK," I said, wondering what the big deal was. I grabbed a hold of the wire and looked up at him.

"Well, I'll be darned. Don't you feel anything?"

"Just a little tingle."

"Well, I'll be darned," he repeated while scratching his head.

That evening at the supper table, he made a big deal about my grabbing the electrically charged wire. "Yeah, he's a real little supercharge," he enthused.

"Supercharge, Supercharge," Roy echoed. That nickname stuck with me until we moved to the farm at Stratton, Colorado. From then on, I was known as Stretch because of my long arms.

I don't recall Dale having a nickname until after we had moved to Colorado. His hairy chest prompted the football players to dub him Hair Bear.

Roy got his nickname via the Shakespearean play, Julius Caesar. We had seen the movie at a drive-in theatre south of Scott City. The next day Roy and I had turned some wooden laths into makeshift swords. I was Marc Antony, he was Brutus. We dueled on top of the haystack, around the trees, and inside of the Quonset. "Dang it, Brutus!" I said as he caught me on the knuckles with his sword.

"Yeah, I'm Brutus, the champion," he taunted.

At supper that evening I absentmindedly said, "Hey Brutus, pass me the bread." I still call him Brutus to this day.

When Janice was little we called her Tish – still do sometimes. She and Anita had a thing going whereby they called each other Fat and Lard, which didn't make sense to me and Roy as they were both on the skinny side.

Nicknames have been a favorite pastime of mine. Witness my family's names: my wife Judy – Rabbit; daughter Sarah – Shoebees or Squeak; Shaun – Swani River, River, or Riv; Mike – Beef or Beefer Weefer; Andy – Bear or Anj.

19 Jumping in the Milo

Sometimes having fun with your siblings wasn't as much fun as it was intended to be. It was fun while it lasted. Everyone laughed and had a good time. No one got mad, and nobody got in a fight. Yet, invariably, someone would get hurt, something would get broken, or something would go wrong.

In the fall of 1951, Dad instructed my brothers and me to help him with the grain harvesting. Dad had a small, flatbed truck that held approximately 100 bushels when the sideboards were attached. In addition to the flatbed truck, he had a new Ford truck, purchased in 1949, with a hydraulic lift that lifted the truck bed up in order to dump the grain.

Dad filled the flatbed truck first with the harvested milo from the combine. He then brought the truck full of grain from the field home to be emptied. After backing the truck into the Quonset building, he took the empty '49 truck back to the field and resume harvesting the grain with his John Deere combine.

In the meantime, Dale, Roy, and I had each been given a scoop shovel to shove the grain off the end of the truck bed onto the concrete floor. Eventually a nice pile of grain began to rise from the floor. We had the truck bed empty and swept off in about thirty minutes.

It would take Dad longer to fill the '49 Ford truck because it had a holding capacity of 200 bushels. While he was filling this truck with grain, Roy and I would shadow big brother Dale as he stalked the shelterbelt with his Red Ryder BB gun looking for sparrows to shoot. Dale was a pretty good shot and he would get a sparrow on every third or fourth attempt. If he was having good luck and feeling like Daniel Boone, then he would occasionally let Roy or me take a shot. We were so excited, the BB gun trembled in our hands. "Aim! Fire!" he would shout out. Sometimes we hit a leaf or twig. It sounded good to us, but Dale would grab the BB gun back, and with an air of authority he would proudly demonstrate the proper technique in shooting a sparrow. Once, Roy actually got a sparrow. We weren't allowed to shoot for a few days after that incident.

We could hear the laboring of the truck engine when Dad arrived with a load of grain. A foot race ensued to see which of us boys would be the first to greet him at the Quonset door. Because of the BB gun, Roy and I usually made sure that we came in second or third. After we had unloaded a couple truckloads of grain, the pile of milo began to grow.

Around noon, Dad arrived with another truck full of grain to be unloaded. When he finished backing the truck into the Quonset, he told us to hurry to the house and get cleaned up for dinner. Following a hearty meal of fried chicken, corn, and mashed potatoes it was time to get back to unloading the truck.

"Hey, you boys get in here and help me!" Dale warned, as he shouted at us from the entrance to the Quonset. Roy and I were busy taunting the chickens by throwing rocks at them. They would scatter in a flurry with their wings flapping frantically. We enjoyed the mad confusion we were creating! It was a challenge to see who could cause the greatest uproar.

Dale was already shoveling grain from the flatbed truck when Roy and I finally arrived. "Wait till I tell Dad that you two were throwing rocks at the chickens," he said.

"We were just having fun," I replied.

"Yeah, just havin' fun," Roy chipped in.

"I don't care! You're supposed to be helping me unload this truck!"

"OK, we won't do it again," I promised.

"Me, too," Roy added.

"Toss your shovels up here, and get busy!"

We pulled our shovels out of the grain pile where we stuck them before going to dinner. We tossed them into the back of the truck and climbed up the side of the bed and pulled ourselves over the side. As I was retrieving my scoop shovel, I lost my footing and fell out rear first onto the pile of grain. It was only a three-foot drop to the grain and it felt like plopping down on a cushion.

"You OK?" Dale asked.

"Yeah," I said, still surprised by the unexpected rush of adrenaline.

Unaware of what was going on because he had his back turned to us, Roy wheeled around with a scoop full of grain and let it fly. I was pelted with grains of milo. "Ouch," I protested as I made a confused attempt to shield my face.

"Oh, I'm sorry," Roy said, with an ornery grin spreading across his face.

Picking up on my discomfort, Dale joined in. "Looks like fun to me," he exhorted as he tossed a shovel full of grain at me. I tried ducking to one side or the other as shovels of grain came hurtling towards me.

Dale and Roy's laughter was contagious. They were having so much fun that their shovels were only half-full when they tossed the grain at me. And I was having fun sprawling around in the pile of grain trying to avoid the flying grain. "Hey," I chuckled, "why don't you guys bury me up to my neck in milo?"

"Yeah," Dale said, "just like covering you with sand!"

Dale and Roy began to fling shovelful after shovelful of milo at me. Soon my legs were covered up to my waist, which didn't take too long because I was sitting down. All of a sudden, I noticed that my arms were beginning to itch. I was having too much fun to let this irritation bother me. I kept hootin' and hollerin' as the grain slowly inched its way up my body.

About the time the grain reached my armpits, Dad arrived with another truckload of grain. Dale and Roy hurried to finish scooping out the rest of the grain from the truck while I struggled to free myself from the pile of grain. After some gruntin' and groanin', I managed to free myself and roll down the pile just as Dad finished backing the truck in.

"What's going on here?" Dad demanded. "How come you're just finishing cleaning the grain out of the truck? And who made this mess in the pile? I bet it was you, Galen."

"Well, I-I-I…"

"Don't 'I' me, mister! What do you think you're doing?

"I-I fell off the truck into the pile," I stammered.

"He did slip off the back of the truck," Dale offered.

"Yeah, fell in," Roy echoed.

"What's the matter with you?" Dad asked me.

"I'm sorry," I pleaded, "don't whip me!"

"No, I mean what's wrong? You're scratching yourself all over."

Because I was afraid of being punished for goofing off, I was unaware of the fact that I was indeed scratching myself all over in a frantic, uncontrollable manner. "Something must have bitten me," I cried out.

"Naw, it's probably just that fine black pig weed seed that gets harvested in with the milo," Dad comforted me while inspecting me. "It bothers me too when I'm running the combine. You're probably allergic to it. I tell you what. Run up to the house and tell Mom to fix you a nice hot bath."

I ran to the house scratching like crazy. That stuff was driving me nuts! "Mom! Mom!" I cried out as I let the screen door slam behind me.

"Whoa! And just where do you think you're going, young man?"

"Dad said you should hurry and make me a hot bath cause I got pig seed on me!"

"Slow down! You got what on you?"

"I fell in the milo and got pig seed on me!" The itching was becoming unbearable.

"Oh, I see," Mom said as she looked at my arms and started to unbutton my shirt. Some grains of milo fell to the kitchen floor. "Pig weed seed," she corrected. "Let's hurry to the bathroom. I'll start the water while you get undressed."

I hopped into the tub and submerged myself up to my neck. It felt so good! But in a matter of moments the itching returned full force. "Help Mom! It still itches!"

"I'm coming." After Mom arrived she handed me a bar of soap and a washcloth. "Scrub yourself real good with this soap and maybe the itch will go away."

While I was lathering and scrubbing myself with soap the itch seemed to go away, but the moment I stopped the urge to scratch my skin off returned. Mom returned, beckoned by my whiny complaints. This time she added some bubble bath to the water and told me to keep scrubbing with soap. Although this helped the itch subside somewhat, the constant irritation was still there. My arms, chest, and back were beet red from all of the scratching and rubbing.

Mom finally ordered me out of the bathtub. After I had toweled myself dry, Mom gently rubbed a skin lotion on my affected areas. She had me assist her in the kitchen with the preparation of the evening meal to keep me occupied. Just thinking about that ordeal still gives rise to an unsolicited itch.

20 Queenie

"What'd you get in that present, Galen?" Roy asked.

"I got that doctor's kit I wanted," I replied. "What'd you get in that present you just opened?"

"A Roy Rogers lunchbox."

"Hey, you boys better come outside and look at these tracks," Dad interrupted, "they might have been made by Santa's reindeer."

Roy and I dropped our presents and ran outside where Dale was already standing beside Dad. Dale was pointing excitedly to a set of tracks that appeared to be running along the side of the house.

"Where's the reindeer?" Roy asked.

"Santa Claus came last night, so I don't think we'll see any of his reindeer Roy," Dad answered.

"Well, who cares about his tracks then?" Roy demanded.

Dad gave Roy a puzzled look and explained, "Santa usually just lands on the rooftops of houses; however, if he has something that is too big or is alive, then he lands on the ground and leaves it in a special place."

Dale, who was growing impatient with Roy's line of questioning, interjected firmly, "Let's follow these tracks around the house and see where they lead to."

"Yeah," I said, "let's go!" We followed the tracks carefully around the house to the north side. As we rounded the corner of the house, we suddenly froze in our tracks. A beautiful horse, mostly white with a brown patch on its forehead and left hip, stood tethered to a cottonwood tree a short distance away. The horse perked its ears up while it munched on a clump of hay. "Wow, did Santa bring us a horse?" I exclaimed.

"It looks like it," Dad said as he untied the bridle from the tree. "Look! There are more tracks leading to the shed."

We followed Dad, who was leading the horse at a safe distance – we weren't quite sure what we were supposed to do. When we reached the shed, Dad handed the reins of the horse to Dale while he opened the shed door. There, sitting on the floor in the middle of the room, was a nice leather saddle and a saddle blanket.

"How comes Santa didn't put the saddle on the horse?" Roy asked.

"Yeah," I echoed, "and what's its name?"

"Slow down you two," Dad said. "Santa probably didn't leave the saddle on the horse for two reasons. First of all, you only put a saddle on a horse when you're going to ride it. Second, if it would have snowed last night, the moisture from the wet snow could have ruined it because it would have caused the leather to shrink. Now, about the name. This paper was attached to the horse's bridle when I discovered it this morning while you boys were busy opening presents." Dad then handed the folded piece of paper to Dale to read to us.

"It says that the horse is a girl and her name is Queenie," Dale stated. We were impressed! The name sounded very regal.

Over the ensuing months, when the weather permitted, Dad instructed us on the proper care and handling of the horse. Queenie was already broken to ride, so our lessons in riding techniques began in earnest. The novelty of having a horse to ride soon faded for Dale and Roy, but not for me. I was now living my fantasies to the fullest. Most of the time I was my hero Gene Autry, riding into the sunset on his horse, Champ. At other times, I was a Pony Express rider or a knight in shining armor.

The dog days of summer left the pasture dry and parched, so Dad opted to herd the dairy cows in the road ditches surrounding the farm. These ditches were always full of green, edible weeds. We boys were assigned the task of herding the cows with Queenie. After a couple of days Dale and Roy conveniently found more important tasks to occupy their time. I didn't mind though, I could now pursue my fantasies every day. One day I'd be herding them along the Chisholm Trail, the next day would be round-up time, and yet another day would be devoted to protecting them from cattle rustlers.

To help with the problem of keeping the stragglers in tow, I crafted a lance out of a split piece of 2 X 4 that I had found behind the shed. It was approximately six feet long. I took Dad's wooden plane and smoothed off the rough edges along the length of my makeshift lance. The next step was to make a sharp point on one end with the bench grinder on Dad's workbench. I also used the bench grinder to smooth the opposite end of the lance for a grip to hold. The lance served me well in my attempts to keep the cows in line or bring them in for water or milking. Most of the time the lance lay cradled in front of the saddle horn on the horse, ready for use when a crisis developed.

My only near-accident occurred late one afternoon as I headed out to round up the cows for their appointed milking time. Roy and I were so engaged in one of our classic Red Sox/Dodgers baseball games that I failed to hear Dad's instructions to round up the cows. However, his third call came as a warning, "Galen! Get the horse and get those milk cows in here, now! I'm not going to tell you again!"

"I think Dad's mad at you," Roy said, dropping the bat.

"Yeah, you're right. Here, put the gloves, bat, and baseball in the shed, OK?" I ran to the barn, grabbed the bridle, and hurried to the corral to corner Queenie. After I put the bridle on her, I led her to the barn where I hastily threw the saddle blanket on her back and placed the saddle on top of it. I fastened the cinch as quickly as possible and then I put my left foot in the stirrup, grabbed the saddle horn, and hoisted myself onto Queenie's back.

I opened the gate and headed down the pasture at a full gallop to round up the milk cows. About halfway down the pasture I suddenly found myself viewing the underside of the horse. In my haste to get Queenie saddled, I had failed to cinch the saddle on properly, and when it loosened from the galloping motion, gravity took over. Fortunately, I was able to jerk my feet free from the stirrups and I let go of the saddle horn. My back hit the ground with a thud and Queenie's two back hooves left an imprint on my thighs as she galloped over me.

Except for some scrapes on my back and some bruises on my thighs, I was OK. After I had fallen off, Queenie halted thirty feet away and was calmly nibbling on some grass. I had no problem catching her and putting the saddle back on her – this time, properly. I then proceeded to bring the cows in for their milking.

It was during this summer of herding the cows that I accidentally discovered Queenie's most unique talent. I had been trying to chase a stubborn calf into the open barn door when it suddenly dodged to the right. I pulled back on the reins hard to get Queenie to stop, but she planted her rear legs and reared straight up in the air with her front legs tucked under her. After I recovered from the shock, I was exhilarated! I was now emulating the Lone Ranger and Silver! All I now had to do to get Queenie to rear up was to gallop towards something and pull back hard on the reins – what a thrill!

One afternoon when I rode into the farmyard, I noticed Roy, Anita, and Janice playing on the north side of the garden. It was time to showcase my Lone Ranger talent. I galloped Queenie towards them. As I approached, they jumped up screaming and huddled together in hysterical fashion. I pulled back hard on Queenie's reins and she responded by rearing straight up in front of them. I triumphantly yelled out, “Hi Yo Silver, away!”

Mom was picking vegetables in the garden. She heard the commotion and witnessed the entire scene. I was told in no uncertain terms to, “Just wait until your father gets home!”

The whipping after supper with the rubber strap from Dad stung and caused the tears to flow, but it was only temporary. I was also restricted from riding Queenie for a month except for herding or rounding up the cows.

Later that evening as we were getting ready for bed, Roy sympathized with my plight and said in a consoling tone, “I’m sorry you got a spanking Galen. Even though you scared me with the horse, you were just like the Lone Ranger.” Sometimes the pain was worth it.

21 Santa Claus

One of the most important events in your life when growing up is your birthday. Not only do you get all of those birthday presents and cards, but you also get treated extra special for a day – especially by Mom. Awaiting the arrival of the Easter Bunny at Easter and sharing in the big feast on Thanksgiving Day were important, too. But the best time of the year was Christmas! Santa Claus was coming!

Roy and I spent countless hours going through the toy section of the Sears & Roebuck and Montgomery Wards catalogs. We always had a rather lengthy list for Mom to forward to the North Pole for us. We usually changed our minds at least twice a week, but Mom never complained about receiving the updated lists. Her only stipulation was that we had to include some clothing items on our lists. We never complained at her suggestions – as long as our lists got to the North Pole. The week before Christmas was the final deadline for any changes we wanted to make on our lists. Mom said that it would take at least a week for our lists to reach the North Pole.

It took us a few Christmases, but Roy and I finally figured out that if we chose different toys we would have more of them to play with. The downside of this game plan was the fact that we often wanted to play with the same toy at the same time. I could usually get Roy to let me play with the toy that I wanted by convincing him that another toy was better. Sometimes he would be real stubborn and I'd have to settle for second choice.

Dad was a stern disciplinarian. But he was also a softy. When it was deemed the proper time to reveal the true identity of Santa Claus to us, Dad passed the buck. About a week before Christmas when I was in the third grade, Dale broke the news to me. I wasn't shocked by this revelation because I had observed Mom hiding packages in the closet. Not only that, when we went shopping in Scott City or Garden City every store seemed to have a different looking Santa Claus. Cousin Billy had also proclaimed his disbelief in Santa the year before. Everyone in the class had scorned him at the time.

We had just finished milking the cows one morning a few days before Christmas. I had picked up a couple of buckets of grain to take to the calves when Dad called me aside. "Galen, you're in the fourth grade now, so it's your turn to break the news about Santa Claus. I want you to tell Roy when you're doing chores this evening after school."

"OK," I said, "how come Dale isn't going to? He told me last year."

"Because it's your turn. Next year Roy has to tell Annie." It made sense to me. Then Annie would have to tell Jan. I then wondered whom Jan would get to tell – maybe Dash. She thought he was her dog anyway.

I had a hard time keeping this important news from Roy that day at school. All the guys in my class had been making fun of the younger kids who still believed in Santa for days. Roy was very adamant in his belief and refused to listen to any of the arguments that were being put forth. I should have gotten a clue from his stubbornness that I was in for a difficult time. Instead, I was relishing the opportunity to play the know-it-all big brother that evening.

After we had finished milking the cows that evening, Dad nodded for me to begin my assigned task. I tried coaxing Roy into helping me feed the baby calves.

"I don't want to," he said.

"But I need help," I pleaded.

"It's too cold out."

"I'll help you the next time you need help."

"I don't care. It's too cold. I'm going to the house."

I started to panic. Dad was counting on me. "I know," I said, "I'll give you that penny I won from you a couple of days ago."

"OK, but you also have to give me your dessert tonight."

Boy he was driving a hard bargain. I was used to always being on the receiving end of our deals. "OK," I said. I had been waiting all day to break the news about Santa Claus to him. After all, it wasn't often that we got to do an approved adult thing.

"Uh, Roy," I said as I started feeding the calves.

"What?" he replied as he trailed along behind me.

"Do you remember what some of the guys have been teasing you about at school?"

"Teasing me about what?"

"You know, that there's no Santa Claus."

"Yeah, so what? They're wrong."

"No they're not. There's no Santa Claus."

"You're a big liar! There is too a Santa Claus!"

"No, there's not. Dale told me last year."

"You're a big, fat liar. How does he know?"

"Dad told him."

"You're all liars!" he screamed as he shoved me backwards. The grain from the buckets that I was carrying scattered all over the ground. "I hate you! I hate all of you!" I could hear wild sobbing as he headed for the house.

"What's all that commotion?" Dad said as he came running over to me.

"Roy got mad when I told him that there was no Santa Claus."

"You didn't tease him about it did you?"

"No I didn't. I tried to tell him just like Dale told me."

"I better catch him before he upsets Mother and the girls," Dad cautioned.

Roy would have nothing to do with me for the next couple of days. I tried being extra nice to him. I even offered to give him a nickel, but to no avail. Finally, while we were opening up our Christmas presents, he became his old self again.

Ironically, he got in trouble the following Christmas when it was his turn to inform Annie about Santa Claus. He really played his informant role like a big shot. Dad even had to resort to using his strap.

22 Accident Prone

"Mommy! Mommy! Roy is hurt!"

"Mommy! Mommy! Anita is hurt!"

"Daddy! Daddy! Janice is hurt!"

Our parents heard these startling, heart-stopping declarations many times when we were growing up on the farm in western Kansas. And when you live ten miles from the nearest medical facility without any telephone service, a sense of impending urgency compounds the situation.

DALE

Brother Dale, the oldest, was probably the most safety-conscious of us kids. However, he too had his moments of physical trauma. Usually, after the excitement had subsided following one of our accidents, Mom and Dad invariably discussed prior mishaps at the supper table.

"I remember when Dale was crying bloody murder when he got the gash on his forehead when he fell on the one-way disc," Dad would begin.

"Yes," Mom would add, "I remember the blood streaming down his face when you carried him into the house. I was simply terrified. Fortunately, it only took a couple of stitches."

Apparently, Dale was pretty young, because the rest of us couldn't recall the incident. Our first realization that we could get injured, not counting deserved spankings, occurred one summer evening shortly before suppertime. Roy and I were helping set the table when Dad came bursting through the screen door carrying a sobbing Dale in his arms.

"Mom, get some gauze and tape!" Dad shouted as he carried Dale towards the kitchen sink.

"What happened?" Mom asked, her face pale.

"Dale stepped on a nail in a 2 X 4," Dad replied. He sat Dale down near the kitchen sink with his legs dangling over the edge of the sink. He quickly untied Dale's shoe, loosened the shoestring, and as gently as possible removed the shoe from the injured foot. Dale's sobbing turned hysterical when he saw his blood-soaked sock. Dad tried to comfort him while he attempted to remove the sock in order to examine the injury. After Mom returned with the gauze and tape, she cradled Dale's head next to her heart and his hysterics soon turned into muffled sobs as she consoled him with words of encouragement.

Dad quickly rinsed Dale's foot off in water, wiped his foot dry with a towel, and wrapped it with gauze and tape. Dad then rushed Dale to the hospital emergency room in Scott City while Mom nervously tended to the rest of us.

"Is Dale going to die?" Roy inquired of Mom, with a worried look on his face. I was pondering the same thought myself.

"Oh no, Roy," Mom said, "Dale's going to be just fine. We just want to make sure his foot doesn't get blood poisoning from the rusty nail." She gave him a big hug and told us to get ready for supper. I remember Roy and I just picked at the food on our plates, something that Mom would have usually scolded us for – but not tonight.

ME

As a skinny kid with gangly arms and legs, I was probably the most prone to sustaining bumps, bruises, scrapes, and cuts. I only have vague recollections of the most serious injury I sustained while growing up on the farm – I was only three or four at the time.

Dale had been chasing me through the living room because I had been tormenting him for some reason. A not-so-gentle shove from him had sent my face through a pane glass window on the living room door. My face had a U-shaped cut, which started at one temple, followed my jaw line down my face, across my chin, and back up the jaw line to the temple on the other side of my face. There was also a cut across my upper lip. My parents rushed me to the emergency room for several stitches. My only flashbacks of the incident are lying on the emergency room table with several doctors and nurses hovering around me and sitting at home in the little rocking chair with my face all bandaged up. The doctors told Mom and Dad that because of my young age the scars would disappear as I grew older. I still have a two-inch scar near my left temple area and an inch-long scar on the left side of my chin.

The injury that is most vivid in my memory though, is the one that was the most embarrassing. Grandpa and Grandma Klenke were visiting us one summer from Spearville. Roy and I were becoming pretty adept at riding our bicycles, or so we thought. We couldn't wait to show off our new skills for Grandpa Bill! When we discovered that our grandparents had arrived, Roy and I rushed into the house to greet them.

"Hey Grandpa, come and watch us ride our bicycles!" I yelled.

"Me, too!" Roy said, as we tugged at his shirtsleeves.

"Hold it you two!" Mom warned as she grabbed each of us by an earlobe. "Where are your manners? You haven't even said 'hello' yet."

"That's OK, Louise," Grandpa laughed, "I've been waiting to see these two demons ride."

"Not so fast," Grandma interrupted, "where are my hugs and kisses?"

We tried wiping the mushy kisses off with the backs of our hands as we exited through the screen door with Grandpa in tow. "I don't know about those two sometimes," Mom muttered.

Dad just recently had a long trench silo dug northeast of the house near the barn. The fall ensilage crop of chopped corn would be placed in the silo and then be fed to the cattle throughout the winter months. Roy and I had discovered big thrills riding our bicycles down through the trench silo. The silo was approximately one hundred feet by forty feet, with a sloping depth of twelve feet.

We started our daring race near the entrance to the barn, which was a couple hundred feet from the edge of the silo. On the command of "Ready, Set, Go!" we peeled out on our bikes, pedaling furiously as we headed for the lip of the silo. As we hit the edge of the silo, we soared several feet into the air before we hit the down slope with a thud and squeals of delight. We then used the burst of momentum to propel us across the floor and up the other slope and out of the silo. Our contests were always close unless one of us crashed going down the slope. However, we were getting to be pros, so wipeouts were becoming distant memories.

We escorted Grandpa to the side of the silo near the front edge. "Wait here Grandpa," I said excitedly, "while Roy and I go get our bikes! We're going to start by the barn and race down through the silo for you!"

"Yeah," Roy echoed, "wait here Grandpa!"

"OK," he chuckled, "I'll have a treat for the winners!" We loved Grandpa – he was the best treat master of all!

Roy and I raced to retrieve our bikes from the side of the shed where we had left them when Grandpa and Grandma had arrived.

"Hurry up," I panted.

"Am too!" Roy gasped.

We hopped on our bikes and pedaled quickly to the entrance near the barn. We stopped, turned, and faced our bicycles toward the silo where Grandpa stood waiting for the race to begin. "OK Roy, no cheating!" I admonished. It was very important that I impress Grandpa – he was left-handed like me.

"Me no cheat!" he retorted.

"OK," I said, "Ready, Set"…and I jumped out ahead of Roy, pedaling for all I was worth.

"Cheater, cheater!" Roy screamed in the background. I didn't care. Grandpa was witnessing the greatest race ever! I hit the lip of the silo in a mad dash and went soaring through the air. As I glanced to see if Grandpa was watching me, I didn't realize that I had slightly turned the handlebars on my bike to the left. I was unable to correct this critical mistake before the front tire jammed into the dirt slope of the silo. I went head over bike and sandpapered down the rest of the slope to the bottom. The left side of my face, arm, and leg were scraped raw. My shirt sleeve and pant leg were shredded. The front wheel of my bike looked like a pretzel.

"Galen, are you OK?" Grandpa called out as he came running down the silo to pick me up. I hurt all over. I was sobbing. I was spitting dirt out of my mouth. I was too mad to reply.

Grandpa picked me up as gently as he could and cradled me in his arms. "Boy, you really took a tumble," he said. Roy came bicycling back down into the silo.

"I won Grandpa! Where's my prize!" he gloated.

Grandma scolded Grandpa for allowing such a thing to happen, and Mom oscillated from feeling sorry for me and comforting me, to admonishing me for being a showoff.

Roy bragged to everyone that he won because I cheated. I felt devastated because I failed to achieve my greatest moment of glory in front of my number one fan.

ROY

Roy's injuries were the most notable because he held the record for the most 100 mph rides to the emergency room in the old Packard car – THREE! Most of us kids had only one such ride.

Our favorite neighbors, the Wilkens, had stopped by one evening for a visit. Roy, Duane, and I were playing cowboys and Indians outside in the shelterbelt south of the house when blood gushed forth from Roy's mouth instead of the sound of a gunshot. "What'sa matter?" I asked.

Tears filled Roy's eyes as he cupped his chin and mouth in his hands. "Stay with Roy," I directed Duane as I headed for the house at a dead run. The screen door banged heavily as I rushed into the kitchen. "Hurry, Roy is bleeding from his mouth," I panted.

"What?" came Mom's startled reply.

"Roy's bleeding! We've got to save him!"

"Where's he at?"

"Out by the shelterbelt!" Mom and Alda (Duane's mom) hurried frantically to keep pace with me. We arrived in a matter of seconds to see Roy coughing and spitting up blood. Duane just stood there, spellbound, with his mouth open.

"Oh, my God!" Mom uttered as she grabbed Roy by the shoulders. "Did Galen hit you or knock you down?"

"No! No!" I protested. "We were just playing and he started bleeding."

"Open your mouth, honey. Oh my goodness! His tonsillectomy is not healing properly!" Mom said.

That was Roy's first emergency ride, and by all accounts the one that buried the speedometer on the car.

The second ride was most noteworthy because of the delayed reaction by Roy to his injury. Roy had been chasing baby sister Jan throughout the house because she wouldn't let him play with one of her toys. I was playing with our toy tractors on the kitchen floor when I heard Roy yell at Jan, "Give me that!"

"No, it's mine!" Jan retorted as she slipped through the slightly opened living room door.

She quickly slammed the door shut just as Roy was reaching for her. A pane of glass from the door shattered on the floor.

"What the heck?" I blurted out.

"I'm telling Mom! I'm telling Mom!" Jan shrieked in delight.

Mom came stomping out of her and Dad's bedroom, which was adjacent to the living room. "Alright, what's going on here?" she questioned.

"Roy broke the window! Roy broke the window!" Jan enthused, sounding like a broken record.

Mom quickly grabbed a broom and a dustpan and began sweeping up the broken glass. "What on earth do you think you were doing, Roy? Just wait until your father gets home from work!"

"But Mom, Jan slammed the door on me!" Roy stammered as he held his right wrist in his left hand.

"I'll bet you were chasing her through the house."

"But, but, Mom…"

"Don't 'but Mom' me, mister!"

I was enjoying this interchange very much because I wasn't the one in trouble, when I noticed that Roy's wrist was dripping blood. "Hey, Roy, look at your hand," I interrupted.

Then a bloodcurdling scream reverberated throughout the two-story farmhouse.

Roy's third trip to the emergency room was the result of a friendly game of baseball one evening before supper. Roy was batting, I was pitching, and Dale was playing fielder. We were playing with a wooden croquet ball because we couldn't find our baseball.

After a few missed pitches, Roy cracked a line drive to the outfield opposite of the side Dale was playing. "Hurry, hurry," I screamed. "We can't let him get a homerun!"

Roy rounded third base and headed home. Dale finally ran the ball down, picked it up, and with a pivoting motion hurled the ball towards home plate. I could tell that it was going to be close. Just as Roy was crossing home plate he turned to catch a glimpse of the ball when it struck him square in the middle of the forehead. He crumpled at my feet. "You killed him! You killed him!" I yelled at Dale as I turned and headed for the house to tell Mom.

Roy was OK, except for a few stitches. Mom and Dad did have to keep him awake for several hours to insure that no brain injury had occurred.

ANITA

In 1949, Dad purchased a new Ford truck in order to haul the harvested grain crops – primarily wheat. It was a super truck because it had a power lift that would lift the bed of the truck up to unload the grain.

Roy, Anita, Jan, and I were marveling at the new truck one afternoon when we were playing near the garage. We climbed in and out of the cab and Roy and I even crawled over the side rails to inspect the bed of the truck. In the meantime, Anita had scooted an empty five-gallon bucket near the right front tire. She turned the bucket upside down and stepped on top of it in order to see over the fender and inspect the hood. Each side of the hood had two long parallel slits to insure proper heat ventilation for the engine.

Anita decided to investigate further by running the little finger of her right hand under and along the width of the lower vented slit. A terrifying scream brought Roy and me to the front of the truck bed near the cab. As we peered over the top of the truck bed we noticed that Anita's hand appeared to be caught in one of the vented slits. She was screaming bloody murder.

"Her hand's bleeding!" Roy said, pointing to her.

"I can tell, you moron!" I shouted, shoving him aside.

"What are we going to do? Mom's going to be mad at us," Roy pleaded.

"No she's not. We didn't do it." I scrambled over the side of the truck and dropped to the ground. I rushed to Anita's side. "You OK?" I asked.

She shook her head, sobbing. "It won't come out," she managed to say in between sobs.

Roy hit the ground with a thud. "Go get Mom, now!" I demanded.

"OK," he said as he sprinted for the house.

I put my arm around Anita's waist and tried to comfort her. "You'll be OK, Mom will save you," I tried to say in a brave tone of voice.

This would be the first of two emergency trips for Anita. She had practically cut off the flesh from the knuckle to the fingernail of her little finger. Her finger always looked skinny after that.

One year for Christmas Anita received a cake making kit. The cake pans, although miniature in size compared to Mom's, really worked. Several little packets of cake mixtures were included in the kit. She emptied the contents of one of these packets into one of the little cake pans, poured in some water, and mixed it with a spoon. Mom then baked it in the gas oven for her for a few minutes – and presto – a genuine, though small, cake would be ready to eat.

The cakes were actually pretty good. Roy and I really had to do some backtracking and double-talking in order to sample some of them. It was hard being nice and doing favors just to get a morsel of cake.

One evening Uncle Anthony and Aunt Rose came to visit. They brought our favorite cousins, Billy and Sammy, with them. Their farm was just two miles north of us near Highway 96.

While Roy, Billy, and I were searching for flashlights to do our daring raid of the farm buildings, Anita was entertaining baby sister Jan and cousin Sammy with her cake making skills. After mixing one of her little cakes she opened the oven door and placed it on the rack.

"I'll go get Mommy," Jan offered.

"No!" Annie replied firmly, "I know how to do it!" She pushed a chair over to the stove, climbed on top of it and leaned across the stove to turn the gas knob on for the oven. She got down from the chair, moved it out of the way, and went to the cabinet drawer to search for the box of matches.

"Better let Mommy do it," Jan warned.

"I know how," Annie said confidently, "I saw Mommy do it many times." She struck the match on the side of the box, set the box on the counter top, and opened the oven door to light the pilot light.

Even though we were in the other room searching for flashlights we could hear the whoosh of the explosion as the gas fumes ignited.

"She's on fire!" Sammy hollered.

Mom, Dad, Uncle Anthony, and Aunt Rose rushed into the kitchen from the living room to see what all the commotion was about. They had been engrossed in a game of pinochle.

Uncle Anthony and Aunt Rose stayed with us as Mom and Dad made the emergency run to the hospital with Annie. They returned a couple of hours later with her. Her face and arms had been covered with salve and wrapped in gauze. Fortunately, she only sustained minor first-degree burns and received no scars from the incident. The doctors said it was like having a bad sunburn.

JANICE

Annie and Jan were always pestering us to see our secret hideout. So Roy and I decided on designing an obstacle course for them to negotiate before we revealed our secret hideout. We weren't worried about them messing with our hideout when we weren't around because we had already made plans to move it to another location anyway.

Our obstacle course, though physically challenging, wasn't intended to confuse or cause the girls to become lost. Roy and I would be like the wagon masters of the Old West who led their parties on the Oregon Trail. We, too, would lead our charges to safety.

We began by the kitchen door, circled the house, and headed east through the yard gate towards the large cottonwood tree, which was approximately 150 feet away.

After we arrived at the tree, we took turns swinging on the rope swing, which hung down from a large protruding branch. We swung back and forth, and on the third swing forward we bailed out and tried to land on our feet running.

The next step on the journey to our secret hideout was to stop at a line we had marked in the dirt, pick up one of the rocks we had placed there, and throw it in the cow tank some twenty feet away.

A short run brought us to the door on the north side of the farm garage. We entered through this door and exited out the west end of the open garage door.

Our next stop was the new chicken coop, which was slightly southwest of the garage. The eave of the roof on the north side of the chicken coop was five feet from the ground and the slope of the roof was only about twenty degrees. Roy and I placed some hay bales in a step-like fashion next to the coop. We hopped up on the bales, crawled up on the roof, then dashed down the length of the roof and jumped down on an empty fifty-gallon oil drum we had strategically placed there.

After jumping to the ground on the south side of the oil drum, we raced through the shelterbelt of trees to the haystack where Roy and I had dug out a cave for our hideout.

Roy and I made a few trial runs through the obstacle course to ensure our complete satisfaction with it. "I think we're ready for the girls," I said.

"Yeah," Roy enthused, "this is gonna be fun!"

"Let's go up to the house and tell them that we're ready."

I led the way, followed by Annie, and then Jan. Roy brought up the rear to make sure our sisters didn't chicken out.

Annie and Jan had only made a couple of goof-ups by the time we reached the chicken coop. They both landed on all fours when they bailed out of the swing and their rocks only made it about halfway to the cow tank.

I had to grab Annie by the hand to help her get on top of the roof and Roy had to push Jan from behind before she made it. I made a dash down the length of the roof, hopped on the oil drum, and jumped down on the south side of the drum. Annie followed suit. Jan was doing fine until she jumped down on the north side of the oil drum. She impaled both of her feet on rusty nails that were sticking up through a decaying piece of lumber.

"Ouchie! Ouchie! Ouchie!" she sobbed.

I ran the short distance back to the garage where Dad was fixing a flat tire. "Hurry Dad," I shouted, "Jan jumped on some nails!" Dad dropped the tire iron and rushed after me to Jan.

"Oh my God!" Dad exclaimed when he got to Jan. He put his size twelve cowboy boots on each side of the board and yanked Jan's feet one by one from the nails that held them. He then picked her up, cradled her in his arms, and ran to the house.

Roy, Annie, and I stood transfixed by the sight of the bloodstained nails that had pierced Jan's feet. "I bet we're going to get it this time," I fussed.

"Yeah, me too," Roy added.

"It's you guys' fault," Annie stammered, "you made us do it."

"Yeah, yeah," was all I could muster in reply.

"Mind your brother Dale," Mom yelled at us as Dad handed Jan to her in the front seat of the car. In a matter of moments the Packard went squealing sideways down the gravel road.

One rusty nail had completely pierced Jan's foot and the other rusty nail almost had. The doctor had to lance it all the way through to help prevent infection.

Fortunately no bones had been broken, which later prompted an analogy with Christ's crucifixion. Jan had her way for several weeks until Roy and I finally got fed up with the whole routine.

23 Hired Help

Bill Lamb was our favorite hired help – at least he was for us boys. We shared the same upstairs bedroom with him, and he had his own radio! We often fell asleep listening to the popular music of the day. Sometimes he took us for rides or played games with us. We felt like we had lost a big brother when he decided to join the Navy. Bill was from Missouri and his sister helped Mom out for a time with us kids. After his stint in the Navy, Bill settled in Connecticut and began a paint contracting business.

Let's face it, with five children and less than six years separating the oldest and youngest, help was needed! The need for help lessened year by year as we grew up and were trained to do the various chores and duties associated with a farm.

Our favorite housemaid was one of my classmates' oldest sister, Evie Kreutzer. Her wedding day on a Saturday morning one bright summer day would result in an emotional scolding from Mom and a whipping from Dad. The problem began during the winter when I was allowed to spend an evening with Bobby after school. After playing outside until it got too dark to see, we decided to resume our activities in Bobby's room. As we were passing through the living room, Evie stopped us and asked me if my brother Roy and I would serve Mass with Bobby at her wedding in the summer. I said, "Sure."

Three or four months later the wedding day arrived. Dale was old enough at the time to be placed in charge of us kids for the morning while Mom attended Evie's wedding in Marienthal. Dad was busy tending to his irrigated crops. When Dad came home for the noon meal, he hollered at Roy and me to come in and get cleaned up for lunch. We had a hot Red Sox/Dodgers game going on at the time.

We had just sat down at the table when Mom walked into the kitchen. She was visibly shaken and tears trickled down her cheeks. She stared at me and in a choking voice asked, "Galen, were you and Roy supposed to serve Mass at Evie's wedding today?"

I was caught off guard. I was dumbfounded. I didn't know what to say. "I dunno," was all I could muster.

"Don't lie to me young man! I've never been so humiliated in all my life!"

"I don't remember. Honest, I don't Mom," I stammered.

Mom then proceeded to recount the whole incident for Dad. "Come here Galen," Dad shouted as he grabbed me by the arm and dragged me across the floor to the whipping chair.

I knew I was in for an extra dose of swats from Dad because he came unglued whenever any of us upset Mom. "Please Dad, I didn't do nothing wrong," I pleaded. My begging was to no avail. I had to use a cushion to sit down on for the next couple of days. Later that evening Roy asked me if we were supposed to serve at the wedding or not. "I don't think so," I said.

"Maybe Bobby forgot to ask you," Roy offered.

"Hey, I bet you're right! It's all Bobby's fault!"

I had a hard time falling asleep because of the shock and pain of the ordeal I had just gone through. Before I finally fell asleep, I had a sudden vision of Evie asking me if Roy and I would serve Mass at her wedding. I not only brought shame and embarrassment to my mother, but I also cost Roy and me fifty cents each – the going rate for serving at a wedding Mass. It would be several weeks before

Bobby would quit taunting me with the extra dollar he made for serving at the wedding by himself. I don't think my apology to Mom the next morning helped ease the tension much.

Another girl, Leslie, also helped Mom with us kids. Mom liked her, but there was a great deal of friction between her and Bill. It reached the boiling point one evening when Mom and Dad were gone. A shouting match ensued between the two of them and Bill kept all of us kids in our bedroom until Mom and Dad returned. Although we boys sided with Bill, we had no idea how the fracas turned out.

One of the most interesting characters to help on the farm was an Englishman by the name of Colin Viner. Colin had been selected by his country to be an agricultural exchange student to the U.S.A. He had read about Dad's irrigation operation in a leading farm magazine and wrote to Dad inquiring about the possibility of helping out on the farm for the upcoming summer months. Dad was so intrigued by the letter that he wrote back inviting Colin to come work for us on the farm. We picked Colin up from the train station in Garden City several weeks later in late spring.

We were all fascinated with Colin's English accent. In addition, as we would soon discover, the meaning of certain words didn't quite match up with ours. A few days after he arrived on the farm, Colin came bursting into the kitchen while Roy and I were helping Mom with the dishes. "Mrs. Conrardy? Bernard needs a torch!"

"What?" Mom said in alarm.

"Bernard needs a torch right away!"

"A torch?"

"Yes! Please hurry!"

"A torch? I don't understand."

Colin finally recognized the confusion etched on Mom's face. He then mimicked holding a flashlight and shining it about.

"Oh, you need a flashlight," she sighed in relief.

The first morning that Colin ate breakfast with us Mom politely asked if he would prefer coffee, milk, or orange juice to drink. He promptly announced that he would prefer tea. Although Mom seemed puzzled by this request, she returned shortly with a nice glass of iced tea. "Oh no," Colin gasped, "could I please have some hot tea in a cup." We had just been introduced to another cultural difference.

Roy and I liked to tease Colin when Mom and Dad weren't around. Even though we loved teasing Colin, we respected the fact that he never told on us like our sisters did. One afternoon Dad had Colin doing some repair work on a farming implement called a disc on the south side of the machine shed. Roy and I were on our way to gather eggs from the chicken coop when we noticed Colin working on the disc. "Hey, Roy, let's sneak around the shed and scare Colin."

"Yeah! Let's scare him good! What are we gonna do?"

We peeked around the edge of the building. "I know, let's throw some rocks on the end of the disc and see if we can scare him!"

"Boy, I bet he gets mad!"

"I wonder if he'll cuss at us in English?" I mused as I picked up some small rocks.

"Who gets to throw first?"

"Go ahead Roy. See if you can hit one of those metal discs." Roy's throw was short and my toss went over the disc.

"What's that?" Colin said in a startled voice. Roy and I giggled as we hid behind the building.

"He doesn't know who did it!" Roy laughed.

"Yeah, or what it was!"

"Let's do it again!"

"OK, but this time we'll both throw our rocks at the same time. Colin's looking the other way. Let's do it!" Our rocks hit two of the metal discs at the same time and a loud metallic ringing noise echoed off the Quonset. Colin jumped into the air and dropped the grease gun he was using.

"Somebody's shooting at me!" he cried out. Roy and I burst into a fit of laughter.

"Ye little devils!" Colin exclaimed as he spotted us. He chased us all over the farmyard yelling the same refrain over and over, "Ye little devils! Ye little devils!"

Another strange incident occurred when we returned from grocery shopping with Mom in Scott City. After we helped Mom carry the groceries into the house, Roy and I took our sunflower seeds and headed outside to do some exploring. We encountered Colin working near the shed and asked him what he was doing. He noticed us eating sunflower seeds and asked us what we were eating.

"Sunflower seeds," I replied, "want some?"

"You're kidding," he said. "Let me see!"

I handed him my sack of seeds to inspect. He shook a few seeds in his hand and studied them carefully. Suddenly, he began laughing uncontrollably.

"What's so funny?" I asked.

"Yeah, what's so funny?" Roy demanded.

"It's, it's the sunflower seeds!" Colin stated between fits of laughter.

"Sunflower seeds taste good," Roy added.

"Yeah, why do you think they're funny?"

"Because, we feed them to our cattle in England."

Colin's experiences on our farm must have been impressive to him because he still sends Mom a Christmas card and note every year.

24 Prayer Life

A farm family in the 1940's and 50's worked together, ate together, and prayed together. Family prayer was the Alpha and the Omega of the day. We prayed before and after every meal. Attendance at Mass was required in the morning before school started, on Sundays, and all Holy Days of Obligation. And during the Lenten season and the month of May (Mary's month) we said the family rosary every evening. In addition, we were encouraged to carry our beads with us and to meditate on a decade or two of the rosary whenever we had a chance.

The first thing we did in the morning after being awakened by Mom or Dad's call to breakfast was to kneel by our bedsides and recite the Guardian Angel prayer, the Our Father, Hail Mary, and Glory Be prayers. When the winter season came we usually gave lip service to our prayers as we rushed down the stairs to the warmth of the living room. Our upstairs bedrooms were without heat. Sometimes Mom would question whether we had actually said our prayers.

Our evening prayers were almost identical to our morning prayers. We knelt by the side of the bed and said our prayers before hopping into bed. Our prayer recitation was more fervent in the evening because we were a little apprehensive of what might happen while we were sleeping. We asked our guardian angels to watch over us in the evenings and to guide and protect us during the day. In our evening prayers we also asked the Lord's blessing on our family, friends, and all those in need.

Before each meal we asked for God's blessing for the food we were about to eat, and after each meal we thanked God for the food we had eaten.

Roy and I were not only curious about our guardian angels, we were also confused about the nature of their existence. To aid in quelling classroom disturbances, Sister told us to be quiet as our guardian angels were sitting on our desktops watching over us. This cautionary warning worked for a few days.

"Billy Conrardy! Stop talking to Bobby! You're making your guardian angel very unhappy. You'd better tell him you're sorry," Sister warned.

"I can't."

"Why not?"

"Because he's visiting with Galen's angel." Giggles came from the class.

"Perhaps you'd better tell him to come and stand guard over you in the corner until recess."

When we were in the fourth through sixth grade classroom, Sister Alberta informed us that our guardian angels were not only invisible, but that thousands of them could sit on the head of a pin at the same time. We were overwhelmed by this statistic. It was unfathomable.

"How can all those angels sit on that pin?" Roy asked me when we were doing chores that evening.

"I don't know. How can they protect us if an ant is hundreds of times bigger than they are?"

"Maybe they're strong like Mighty Mouse."

"Yeah, but Mighty Mouse is a big mouse. I think Sister is pulling our leg, she just wants us to be good."

When Roy asked Sister what our guardian angels' names were, she said that they were the same names as our middle names. Hence, Roy's was Eugene, and mine was Bernard. However, Sister didn't believe that Dale's middle name, Elmer, was a saintly name. So his third name, William, which had been added on his baptismal record, was the name of his guardian angel.

One of our most enjoyable prayer sessions occurred during our last Lenten season at Marienthal before we moved to the farm in eastern Colorado. Father Reif invited several of the area priests to participate in the singing of the Litany of the Saints. Roy and I were fortunate enough to be chosen to serve for this Lenten service. After the initial introductory prayers, the priests joined voices in singing the praises of the saints.

They chanted, "Sancta Angelina."

The parishioners responded, "Ora pro nobis."

..."Sancta Anastasia."

... "Ora pro nobis."

... "Sancta Antonio."

... "Ora pro nobis."

It was uplifting and upbeat, considering the penitential nature of Lent.

During that same Lenten season, Mom took Anita and Janice to a birthday party for one of their friends. While Dale helped Dad with the newborn calves, Roy and I were to do the supper dishes and to pray the rosary. After everyone had gone, Roy complained, "Boy, this is going to take forever. We hafta wash the dishes and then dry the dishes and put them away. And then we still hafta pray the rosary by ourselves."

"I know what. I'll kneel down and lead the rosary while you wash the dishes. That way we'll be done in half the time."

"OK, let's get started."

I dug the rosary out of my pocket, knelt down, made the sign of the cross, and began leading the recitation of the holy rosary. We never missed a beat and Roy responded on cue. The first two decades of the Sorrowful Mysteries of the rosary went by in a matter of minutes. While we recited the last three decades of the rosary, Roy managed to dry the dishes and put them away.

"That last part of the rosary sure took a long time," he said.

He was right. I had thrown in several extra Hail Mary's with the last three decades. Timing was everything. Besides, we were supposed to gain some kind of indulgences by saying extra prayers. These indulgences were supposed to help us get out of Purgatory quicker after we died. You had to go to Purgatory to get totally cleansed of all your sins before you could go to Heaven. Purgatory sounded like a scary, dark, lonely place. I already knew that Roy and I could use all the help we could get...

25 Little Moron Jokes

We attended a small school in the town of Marienthal, population fifty. Actually, there were two small schools. The little one-room building was located a few hundred yards just southeast of the Catholic Church. Grades one through three were educated there. The big schoolhouse, consisting of two classrooms, was approximately a block and a half north of the one-room building. In all, some sixty students attended grades one through eight.

We were a public school under the auspices of Wichita County, but we were taught by the Precious Blood nuns out of Wichita. Most everyone thought we were a parochial school. Our school day always started with seven o'clock Mass at Immaculate Heart of Mary Church. Then we were herded to our respective school buildings. After the Pledge of Allegiance, classes began in earnest. Of course, the best part of the school day was morning and afternoon recesses, followed closely by noon lunch.

My older brother, Dale, my younger brother, Roy, and I had all "graduated" from the little school to the big house. Dale was in the east room of the building for seventh and eighth graders; Roy and I were on the west side with the fourth through sixth grades.

Sister Alberta was our teacher. She was on the plump side, wore glasses, and generally had a good sense of humor. However, she could break our eardrums if she were angry with us. She had a really husky voice! She always said we boys would be the death of her. We wondered who would be naughty enough to do such a thing. The nuns fascinated us. They were always dressed from head to foot in black and they wore white, starched bibs around their cheeks and necks. And they had strong arms and hands! They sure could swing a mean ruler across our knuckles!

No one really knew how Sister Alberta got her nickname, Sister Gertie, but it fit. The year Roy made it into the fifth grade, Sister Gertie informed the classes at the beginning of the school year that we would celebrate each student's birthday. Each birthday was celebrated during the last fifteen minutes of the school day. The celebration began by singing Happy Birthday to the birthday student. The honored student would then have to sing back, "I thank you I do, I thank you I do…" I hated birthdays at school – especially when mine came around. There was a five-minute entertainment period before the cupcakes, cookies, and Kool-Aid were served by the birthday person. Sister Gertie had determined that this school year the honored birthday student would also perform the entertainment, which consisted of telling two jokes in front of the classroom. Boy, did I hate birthdays at school!

It was the day of Roy's birthday celebration. Sister Gertie announced the homework assignment for each class and then called Roy to the front of the classroom. He looked so innocent standing there, his cowlick combed neatly back, his bib overalls covering up the front of his Roy Rogers shirt, and his hands stuffed in his pockets. Sister Gertie joined in the hearty rendition of Happy Birthday, and Roy sheepishly sang off-key the reply of, "I thank you I do." It was embarrassing!

"What kind of jokes are you going to tell us?" Sister Gertie asked the birthday boy.

"Little Moron jokes," came the reply.

"Please Lord, not the Little Moron jokes," I pleaded in silence.

"Go ahead, Roy," Sister said.

"Do you know why the Little Moron flushed himself down the toilet stool?" Roy inquired of the class. I slowly began to sink in my chair.

"No," a petite red-haired girl in the front of the classroom replied.

"Because his mother called him a turd," Roy grinned. Sister Gertie's face became flush.

"Go ahead and tell us your other joke," she added hesitantly.

"Why did the Little Moron run through the fence?" Roy asked confidently. Silence filled the room.

"Why did he run through the fence?" Sister Gertie finally added. I was now completely huddled under my desk with my hands cupped over my ears.

"Because he wanted to strain his nuts," Roy said, with a huge smile on his face.

The girls didn't really understand, thank God! And the boys, although somewhat stunned, were snickering softly. Sister Gertie's mouth was wide open and she was now beet red. "Let's have some birthday goodies," was all that she could muster.

"How was Roy's birthday party at school?" Mom inquired as I walked through the kitchen.

"Fine," I said as I dashed upstairs.

26 The Finger

It was a typical spring day. The weather was nice, the birds were chirping, and recess never seemed to come. A couple of the stars of our makeshift baseball team (we always did battle with the seventh and eighth grade team) had to stay in during ten o'clock recess because they had failed to turn in their homework assignments. This serious blow to our chances of competing prompted muffled chants of, "Sister Gertie, Six-gun Turdy," as we exited the school building with our baseball gloves and bats. We got our butts kicked, but we vowed revenge.

The rest of the morning classes drug by, with Sister Gertie alternating instruction between three classes. We usually doodled when Sister was preoccupied with one of the other classes. We'd pull out our Big Chief tablets, get our Scripto Eversharp pencils out, and start to mess around. Oftentimes we'd try and pass notes. Usually someone got mad and a spit wad battle ensued. Of course, the primary objective was to not get caught. This morning no one did! Finally, Sister Gertie rang the dinner bell.

The Sisters all went to the nuns' house for lunch. A few of the students who lived in town went home for lunch, but most of us brought our sack lunches to school. It was so nice out that most of us ate our lunches by the merry-go-round on the playground. It was a boisterous, rowdy time! At some point in a young boy's life he is taught, or picks up on, the daring-do of symbolic gestures. It probably got started among my classmates by one of the guys who had an older brother in high school. Flipping the middle finger at one of the upperclassmen, or more especially, the girls, was a defiant thing to do. On this particular day we didn't back off, we really pressed our newfound defiance to the limit. This turned out not to be a good thing to do.

Sister Gertie stood out in the schoolyard and rang the bell three times to signify the beginning of the afternoon classes. Before she could tell the designated class to get out their textbooks, several of the girls approached her for a conference at the front of the room. Judging by their excited whispers and quickly turned heads in our direction, we instinctively knew we were in trouble. A few minutes later Sister Gertie instructed the girls to return to their seats.

With a very stern look on her face, Sister informed us boys that we would be spending recess in the classroom. The afternoon recess began at 2:30 p.m. It came around too quickly. After Sister Gertie had dismissed the girls, she calmly closed the door and walked back to the front of the classroom. A quick glance around at the faces of my classmates revealed that they, too, had a good idea of why we were being detained.

"Boys," she said in a drawn out manner, "the girls have informed me that you have been making some naughty gestures at them." We all looked accusingly at each other. I spotted some paper lying on the floor and I slid out of my desk and busily started picking it up. I really didn't want Sister Gertie to call on me.

After surveying the many guilty faces around the room, Sister exclaimed while demonstrating with her middle finger extended on her right hand, "What does this mean?" There was dead silence. No one moved a muscle. "I said, what does this mean?" she repeated.

I froze. Brother Roy was holding his hand up enthusiastically. We were dead, no doubt about it. I couldn't get his attention. We were dead.

"Yes, Roy?" she said, while gesturing again, "What does it mean?"

Roy, in his baby-faced expression, stood up and boldly declared, "I'm not exactly sure, Sister, but I think it means, 'Stick it up your butt'!"

We lost recess privileges for an entire week. I thought the guys would be mad at my brother. They weren't. They were just happy that they didn't have to answer Sister's probing question. Me, too!

27 Losing Grandpa

Being raised on a farm, we knew that things died. We saw dead baby calves and pigs. We watched Dad shoot pheasants and rabbits. We helped catch chickens, chop off their heads with a hand ax, and clean them for eating. We also saw Dad, with the help of some of his neighbors, kill and butcher steers and hogs.

Roy and I loved to take out rodents and insects. Our favorite species to exterminate were red ants. It was easy to locate their colonies in sand-covered mounds. We swiped some stick matches from the cupboard in the kitchen, found a couple of empty tin cans, and filled them with gasoline from the fuel storage tank behind the shed. We then proceeded to scout the farmyard for our unsuspecting prey. Once a mound was located, we poured gasoline down the entrance hole of the mound and doused the rest of the mound with the gasoline that was left in the can. Then we stood back a few feet, struck the match on a rock, and tossed it onto the mound. Whoosh! Flames shot up and heat gushed outward. The little red ants on the surface of the mound were toasted to a crisp! It was a powerful sight to us. Sometimes we would torture them first by pouring some gasoline around the perimeter of the mound and lighting it. We could see the ants in the inner circle make a beeline for the mound's entrance.

Early one morning while we ate breakfast there was a loud knock on the screen door. Dad got up from the table and went to see what the frantic knocking was all about. "Come on in boys," we heard Dad say. We couldn't understand their muffled replies through the screen door, but Dad went outside and closed the door behind him. In a few minutes Dad returned alone with a strained look on his face.

"What's the matter, honey?" Mom asked with a puzzled look on her face.

"Come into the living room with me," he implored. Mom hurried into the living room with Dad and shut the door behind her. The only thing we could make out was an "Oh, no!" from Mom. They emerged a few moments later. Dad headed for their bedroom and Mom went outside and invited the boys in. It was Jerome and Delbert – Uncle Anthony's boys – who lived on a farm two miles north of us. "Would you boys like something to drink?" Mom asked.

"No thanks, Aunt Louise," they responded politely. They stood there with their caps in their hands and shuffled their feet back and forth as they waited. Dad emerged suddenly from the bedroom all dressed up with a small suitcase in his hand. He gave Mom a quick kiss goodbye, told us kids to behave and mind our mother, and quickly left with our cousins.

"Mom, where's Dad going?" Dale asked, concerned.

"Listen children," Mom said, trying to compose herself, "Daddy's going down to Dodge City to see Grandpa Conrardy."

"What's the matter with Grandpa?" I demanded.

"Well-l-l," she stammered, "he's not feeling well." We didn't pursue the matter. It was obvious that Mom was upset. We could see tears well up in her eyes. We figured Grandpa must be pretty sick for Dad to travel to Dodge. Mom seemed lost to us that day. Roy and I had spilled a drink on the kitchen floor that we were fighting over and Mom wiped up the spill without a word of reprimand.

That afternoon Roy and I were playing baseball when we saw Uncle Anthony's pickup pull into the yard. We saw Dad get out and then the pickup pulled away. Dad ignored our yells of "Hi" and headed for the house instead. Out of curiosity, Roy and I ran for the house. As we entered the kitchen we could see Mom and Dad hugging each other, and they were crying. We had never seen Dad cry before. We had seen Mom cry at Jimmy Stewart and June Allyson movies, so that didn't shock us – but Dad crying! I couldn't take it, I ran upstairs to our bedroom and sat on the edge of our bed and began to weep. Roy came tiptoeing in a few seconds later.

"What's the matter?" he asked gently, putting his hand on my shoulder.

"I don't know," I replied honestly. I just couldn't seem to handle the sight of Dad crying. Later that evening at the supper table Dad informed us children that Grandpa Conrardy had passed away and that we would all be going to Dodge City the next day. That night as we lay in bed Roy wanted to know how Grandpa had passed out. "I guess he must've got hit in the head pretty bad with something and it knocked him out," I replied.

"Is he still knocked out?"

"I guess so."

"Why are we going to see him for, then?"

"I dunno, so we can help him wake up, I guess."

"How are we gonna do that?" he persisted.

"I guess we'll take turns carrying him around. Now get to sleep."

On the way to Dodge in our 1952 Ford car Roy inquired as to what or who had knocked Grandpa out. "I'm sorry Roy, but Grandpa is dead. He died of a heart attack yesterday," Mom said as she turned her head to the back seat. I was stunned.

"Who attacked his heart?" Roy demanded.

"His heart just quit beating," Mom answered.

"Can they get it started again?" Roy asked.

"I'm afraid not," she responded.

We endured the rest of the trip in silence. It usually took an hour and a half to make the trip to Grandpa's farm just east of Dodge City, but it seemed like forever this time. All of the uncles and aunts and their families were there when we arrived just before noon. There sure was a lot of hugging and crying. Roy and I explored Grandpa's farm with some of our cousins so we could avoid the confusion in the house.

That evening at supper, we were told that Grandpa's body would be brought in a casket to the house for a wake the next afternoon. "Who's gonna wake him up?" Roy whispered to me.

"I don't know," I whispered back, "maybe he wakes up when we pray for him." I had heard talk earlier of praying for Grandpa the next day.

Sure enough, the next afternoon a big, black, shiny automobile pulled up in front of the house. The driver and his assistant emerged from the vehicle, both dressed in black suits. They opened the rear doors of the black car and pulled a long box-like thing out that had handle rails along the sides. Dad and some of the uncles helped them carry it into a cove area of the living room. The driver opened the lid up on the front part of the box, and then he and his assistant left.

Later that afternoon it was our family's turn to pray in front of the open casket. Grandpa lie there in his best suit and tie with his hands folded across his chest with his black rosary draped around them. It looked like he was sound asleep to me. Roy tugged at my shirt as we departed to let another family take its turn.

"What?" I asked, irritated by the distraction.

"Did you feel Grandpa's hand?"

"No, why?"

"Boy was it cold!" he said. Our family had another prayer vigil that evening. Roy was right; Grandpa's hand was cold!

The next day was the funeral Mass at St. Andrew's Church in the little town of Wright. The church was packed with relatives and friends. After Mass, the casket was taken to the cemetery across the road for burial. The priest said some more words and then sprinkled holy water over the coffin. Grandma, Dad, and his brothers and sisters also got to sprinkle holy water on it. Some of the family members tossed a rose on the coffin before they departed for the parish hall for the luncheon that had been prepared for the family. Roy, my cousin Billy, and I stayed behind and watched the crew lower the coffin into the grave and begin to shovel dirt on top of it.

"I wonder if Grandpa can feel that?" Billy pondered.

"Yeah!" Roy added.

"I don't think so," I added, "you can't feel anything when you're dead." But, you supposedly went to Heaven sometime after you died. Christ rose from the dead three days after He died. I was hoping that we could stay for three more days so that I could see Grandpa's ghost rise from the grave and go to Heaven with Jesus, but we had to leave the next day for home.

28 Afraid of the Night

Roy and I had to stay at Uncle Adolf and Aunt Lucy's farm when we were in Wright to attend Grandpa Conrardy's funeral. The two-story Conrardy farmhouse wasn't big enough to hold everyone. After the family had recited the evening rosary for Grandpa, our cousin Kevin took us to the farm – he was charged with babysitting us.

After we arrived, Kevin took our suitcase into the bedroom we would be sleeping in, then he took us into the living room. While Roy and I sat on the sofa wide-eyed and gawking at our new surroundings, Kevin went into the kitchen and returned with some milk and homemade chocolate chip cookies – one of our favorites.

"You boys want to hear some scary stories before you go to bed?" Kevin chuckled. We nodded our heads yes. Our mouths were full of cookies and we were too intimidated to say no.

"Well," he began in a reflective mood, "you remember that large shelterbelt we passed on the way home about a half mile north of here?" He didn't wait for an answer. "That shelterbelt is much bigger than the one Uncle Bernard planted at your farm. Ours has five rows of huge trees that stretch for half a mile. It has lots of birds in it – pheasants, quail, meadowlarks, sparrows, and others." Roy and I nodded our heads in agreement because we had seen meadowlarks and sparrows in ours, too.

"But," he said, with that menacing grin returning to his face, "there are other scary creatures in there, too!" Roy and I began scooting towards each other in the middle of the sofa.

"Don't you want to know what kind of spooky animals are in there?" he prodded.

"I-I d-d-don't k-know," I answered feebly. I almost spilled my milk when Roy bumped into my elbow.

"Well, for one thing, there's lots of rabbits," he said. Roy and I managed a grin as we glanced at each other. Heck, we weren't afraid of no rabbits!

"However," he proceeded, "there are some badgers and snakes running and crawling in there." I was deathly afraid of snakes and we knew what a badger was. Roy and I squished a little closer together.

"We don't hafta go in there, do we?" Roy pleaded. "Ouch," he yelled out as I elbowed him in the side.

"What'sa matter Galen, afraid to go in the shelterbelt?" Kevin laughed. Suddenly, he leaned forward in his chair. "What we didn't know," he continued, "was what scary thing was in there at night."

"What was that?" Roy choked as I squeezed his arm.

"Well, I'll tell you," he whispered as he glanced towards the door. "One night I had to go to the outhouse, and it was really dark out. When I got done and closed the door I thought I saw a shadow move on the side of the outhouse." My throat was feeling dry and parched as Kevin squirmed nervously in his chair.

"I turned and headed for the house. I started to walk faster because I could hear footsteps behind me. Something brushed my shoulder – and as I turned to see what it was, this big paw swiped me across the side of my face. How do you think I got these scars?" he asked as he turned his head to the side.

Roy and I were terrified. Our cousin had lived to tell about it.

"Yeah, that bear's still out there. He lives in the shelterbelt at night, you know. Shall we hop in the car and go see if we can find him?"

I jerked Roy off the sofa by the hand and made a mad dash for the bedroom. Roy struggled wildly to maintain his balance.

"I'll tell you what," Kevin said in a hushed tone, "I'll leave a note for Mom and Dad to lock the door when they come home so we'll be safe."

I slammed the bedroom door shut after I had pulled Roy through. We kicked off our new shoes and hastily jumped under the protective covers.

"Me scared!" Roy whimpered.

"Me too!" I replied.

"Please turn the light on!"

"OK." I slipped quietly out from under the covers and flipped on the light switch. I pulled the window shade all the way down and jumped quickly back under the covers with Roy.

The next morning there was a rap on the door. "Time for breakfast, boys," Aunt Lucy said in her pleasant, motherly voice.

Roy and I peeked out from under the covers. It was daylight – we were saved! We learned several years later that Kevin's scars had come from an auto accident.

We were glad to return home following Grandpa's funeral. As we pulled into the front yard Roy nudged me and pointed out the window. "Look," he whispered, "the shelterbelt."

The shelterbelt was one of our favorite places – could it possibly harbor a big, black bear? "Yeah," I replied as I put my arm around him. "We'll be OK as long as we don't go in there at night."

A couple days later, following supper, Mom asked Dad if he could repair her sewing machine. After a quick inspection of the sewing machine Dad told me to go to the machine shed and get his small tool kit off of the workbench for him. "Do I hafta?" I whined.

"Yes, Dale's helping with the dishes, so go get my tools for me – now!"

"OK," I stammered. I turned on the porch light and quietly eased through the squeaking screen door. After I opened the yard gate I crept silently towards the machine shed, which was only a hundred feet southeast of the yard. The shadow cast by the huge cottonwood tree was really spooky and I kept a wary eye on it.

I could feel my heart thumping in my chest as I reached the side of the building. Fortunately for me there was a side door on the northeast corner of the shed that was near the workbench. I opened the door quickly, reached around the corner to flip on the light switch, and retreated a few paces along the side of the building.

Nothing emerged except a burst of light. Slowly and cautiously, I approached the open door. A hurried glance inside of the shed revealed more shadows lurking about. I noticed the tool kit sitting a short distance from me on the workbench. Two giant steps put me in front of the tool kit. I snatched it up, wheeled around, and bounded out of the shed. I slammed the door shut with my right hand as I went through the doorway. Shadows seemed to be closing in on me as I dashed for the house. Suddenly, I could hear panting noises and a rush of footsteps behind me. "Help! Help!" I pleaded as I ran through the yard. I could feel something nipping at my heels as I slid through the screen door. Our dog, Lassie, jumped on the screen door and started barking.

"Dang stupid dog!" I cried out.

Dad reprimanded me for leaving the light on in the shed the next morning.

That summer Dale was a given a big responsibility – babysitting his brothers and sisters for the first time. Mom and Dad were going to a dance in Scott City with the neighbors. Roy and I would rather have had our usual babysitter. Dale was going to be tough, we could tell. However, he didn't say much. When it was 9 p.m. he told us all it was time for bed. He made sure we went to the restroom, washed our hands and faces, and said our evening prayers.

Just before I hopped in bed with Roy, I glanced out of our bedroom window. I was shocked by the bright, glaring light that was reflecting off the barn to the east of the house. "Somebody's here," I yelled at Dale as he entered the bedroom from tucking the girls in bed.

"Nobody's here. Get to bed," he commanded.

"Look! Look!" I pointed at the window.

"I don't see anything."

"Look out the window that way," I said as I frantically pointed with my finger.

"OK, I'll look." He peered out the window in the direction of my frantic gestures. "It does look like something is shining on the side of the barn," he admitted. "Maybe it's the headlights from a car."

"We're going to be robbed and killed!" I screamed.

Dale ran next door to the girls' bedroom and herded them back to our room. "Here, you girls sleep in my bed for a while," he said. "Galen, let's sneak downstairs and get a baseball bat."

"No way!" I screamed.

"Okay, you big baby. Roy, you come with me."

"O-OK," Roy said as Dale grabbed him by the hand. It seemed like hours before they returned. Roy and I huddled together under the covers on our bed; our sisters did likewise in Dale's bed, as he stood watch with the baseball bat.

Some hours later, after Mom and Dad had returned from the dance, they discovered all of us kids in our bedroom. Dale was curled up on the floor with the baseball bat firmly clutched in his hands. "What's going on here?" Dad quizzed as he and Mom awakened us.

Step by step, Dale recounted the whole scenario for them. Dad went to the window and glanced out for a few moments. He began to chuckle. “Come here,” he said. “See, the light that’s reflecting off the side of the barn is coming from the full moon that is shining tonight.”

After Mom and Dad left our bedroom with Jan and Annie, Dale glared at me as he prepared to get into his bed, “We’re gonna be robbed and killed, huh?”

I still get a queasy feeling at nights. The image of that big, black bear still haunts me.

29 Jumping out of the Cottonwood Tree

The best way to deal with the hot summer days of western Kansas was to cool down with water. There were several ways that we could accomplish this: in a rainstorm, by having a water fight, in the irrigation ditch, or by jumping into the cow tank.

We loved running and playing outside when it was raining. The fresh smell of air following a rainstorm was invigorating. However, there were limiting factors to our enjoyment of rain. The biggest problem was that it didn't rain very often in western Kansas. If it did rain, the severe lightning that usually accompanied these storms restricted us to sightseeing from an indoor kitchen window. Or strong, gusty winds would hammer us with sheets of water and force us to seek shelter. When a slow, gentle rain did occur, we were in heaven!

Dale, Roy, and I splashed around the yard barefooted in our bib overalls. In a matter of minutes little pools of water began showing up all over the place. Our favorite trick was to catch each other off guard by jumping into a little pool of water. The splash from the unexpected, cold, wet water took our breath away and aroused the revenge monster. Laughing and splashing we chased each other around the farm. A mud-wrestling contest usually ended the fun in the rain.

"Hey Galen, let's get Roy!" Dale shouted at me.

"OK," I said, "let's get him!"

"Gotta catch me first," Roy laughed as he darted away.

"He's going around the shed," Dale panted, "I'll go around this way, you go around the other way."

"OK," I replied.

When Roy realized that he was going to be caught in a trap he tried to break free, but Dale brought him down with a flying tackle. I jumped on top of them and the free-for-all began. We smeared handfuls of mud in each other's faces and hair with reckless abandonment until the ringing cry of 'BOYS!' broke our concentration. We had to hose each other down with the garden hose before Mom let us enter the house – and then only after a head-to-toe inspection.

One thing we boys enjoyed doing was catching little toads after a nice rain shower. Our jumping frog contests never seemed to turn out the way Mark Twain's did. We thoroughly enjoyed teasing and frightening our sisters with them. They'd yell and scream and run and hide. Of course, Mom was their last line of defense. And she was a formidable one.

Our water fights were more frequent than the rainstorms. Cleaning the dairy barn's concrete floor, watering the garden, or washing one of the vehicles was the catalyst for a good fight. The weapon of choice was always the powerful garden hose. Whoever controlled this weapon was usually the instigator of the water wars and the eventual winner. If all three of us boys were involved, then Dale usually reigned supreme. One time, however, Roy and I gained the upper hand.

We were washing the family car one sunny afternoon when Dale began hosing Roy and me down. "Take that you varmints," he laughed.

"Cut it out," I yelled.

"Yeah, cut it out," Roy complained.

The force of the water from the nozzle kept us at bay, so we ducked around the other side of the car for protection. Dale shot water in a high arc over the top of the car and let the water cascade down on us, and he tried to hit our legs by blasting us under the car.

"What are we gonna do Galen?" Roy implored.

"I dunno. Let me think. Hey, I know! You sneak up to the front of the car and poke your head above the hood of the car. When he sees you, he'll try to squirt you and then you duck back down. You keep teasing him like that while I sneak into the garage and find a bucket to fill up with water. I'll use the water tap inside the garage and then I'll sneak back behind the car, OK?"

"OK," he said, "you promise this is going to work?" I nodded affirmatively.

When Roy had gained Dale's attention, I managed to crawl to the garage without being spotted. After I filled the bucket full of water, I waited at the edge of the garage until I caught Roy's attention. Catching the drift of my gestures, he jumped up in front of the car and double-dared Dale to hose him. I crouched down and scooted to the side of the car unseen. Roy had taken a good drenching to ensure my safety. He crawled around the side of the car to join me.

"Have you had enough, you two babies?" Dale challenged.

"Now wha-wha-what are we going to-to do?" Roy shivered.

"You were really brave," I said encouragingly as I patted him on the back. "Can you go back and do the same thing again?"

"I dunno, I'm cold and wet."

"It's worth one, no, I tell you what, I'll give you two pennies."

"OK. But what are you going to do?"

"While he's busy shooting you with the hose I'm going to sneak up behind him and dump this bucket of water on him."

"Good idea!"

"Let's go."

"I got you again," Dale exclaimed as he aimed the hose at Roy.

"Surprise!" I yelled out as I dumped the bucket of water over Dale's head.

"Hey!" was all he could muster in reply. I dropped the bucket and made a mad dash for the shelterbelt. I managed to stay out of sight until it was time to do the evening chores.

Another way we would cool down was in the irrigation ditches. Dad irrigated corn, alfalfa, and sorghum crops from this water source. The ditches were approximately three and one-half feet in width and two and one-half feet in depth. And they ran over half a mile in length at times. Siphon tubes ran the water down the crop rows. Sometimes thirty or forty rows ran at the same time.

Occasionally Roy and I went a quarter mile or more up the ditch away from the crops being watered and hopped in. The water was ice-cold, but after we caught our breaths, we could float along on the fast moving water.

Our best source of relief from the searing heat was splashing around in a big cow tank. Dad had a spare aluminum cow tank on hand, and our hired hand, Bill Lamb, helped him move it under the big cottonwood tree east of the house. The tree's large branches provided ample shade for us. We ran a garden hose to the tank and filled it to a depth of about two and a half feet. The tank was twelve feet across and the sides were three feet high.

Roy, Anita, Janice, and I splashed around pretending we were world class swimmers. None of us could really swim – but you couldn't tell by our boastful exclamations.

One of Roy's favorite dares, and mine too, was to take a deep breath and see who could stay under water the longest before coming up for air. The advantage usually went to the one who made the initial dare because he would be taking in air while the other one was still contemplating the dare.

"I bet you a nickel I can stay down longer than you can," I challenged.

"Can't neither!" Roy replied.

Several seconds later Roy broke the water's surface ahead of me. "You owe me a nickel," I gasped.

"I want to dare you back."

"No, I want my nickel. I won."

"You just think you're as good as Tarzan."

"Maybe I am."

"OK, I double-dare you to dive from that branch into the tank like Tarzan. And I bet you another nickel that you can't."

There was a large branch extending from the cottonwood tree out over the cow tank. It was probably seven feet high. Roy knew I had a problem with heights. However, a double-dare, coupled with the prospect of winning another nickel, was something that could not be turned down. "OK, you asked for it," I said, "get your nickels ready!"

I climbed up the makeshift ladder attached to the trunk of the tree and slowly made my way up to the branch. I grabbed hold of a smaller branch above me to help guide my shaky steps down the overhanging branch.

"That's far enough," Roy yelled up at me.

I didn't dare look down. "I-I-I know," I said weakly.

"Well, are you going to dive in or not?"

"Wh-when I-I'm ready."

"I double-dare you! I triple-dare you!"

That did it! I put my hands out in front of me in a praying position, bent my knees, and dove headfirst into the tank. As my head hit the water, my hands and arms crumpled beneath me as they hit the floor of the tank. A split-second later, my head followed suit.

"Mom, Galen's drowning!" Annie called out to Mom, who was hanging up laundry on the nearby clothesline.

Mom dropped the laundry basket and came running to the side of the tank. "Oh my gosh," she cried out as she pulled me from the tank. "What happened?" she inquired. A strong slap to the middle of my back started me coughing and sputtering.

"Roy made him do it," Jan offered.

"Made him do what?" Mom said.

"He dared him to jump from that tree branch," Annie added while pointing to the overhanging branch.

"Are you OK, Galen?" Mom asked.

"Yeah, I think so. My head kinda hurts though."

"Let me see. Wow, do you ever have a big knot on your forehead! Let me take you to the house and check this out."

That evening at the supper table Mom and Dad explained to us kids that the cow tank didn't have enough water depth in it to handle such a dive.

"Here's your two nickels Galen," Roy said, "that was a great dive. Just like Tarzan does it. I'm sorry you got hurt."

"That's OK." And I gave him a hug.

30 The Thinker

Peaceful bliss is best described as lying under the shade of a huge cottonwood tree on a farm on a sunny afternoon watching the clouds float by. While some people see animals, birds, or ships in the shapes of the clouds, I fantasized floating on a cloud and viewing far away, exotic places. I visited all those places I read about in books: the mountains, the oceans, and far away places with strange people and customs. My freedom, my escape, my solitude.

I was always being accused of daydreaming, mostly at the supper table. Quite often one of the neighbors would be our guest because he had helped Dad with some fieldwork or harvesting of crops. When supper ended, Dad, Mom, and our neighbor would catch up on the latest local news. It was disrespectful for us kids to leave the table until being dismissed; besides, the discipline chair wasn't far away. It was never long before I was thinking about sailing the ocean or climbing a mountain.

"Galen, time to help with the dishes," Mom said. No reply. "Galen, time to do the dishes!" Still no reply. "Galen, what are you doing?"

"Huh?"

"What's the matter with you? Are you daydreaming again?"

"Ah, no, I don't think so."

"Well, you better start paying attention and help with the dishes!"

Sister Alberta loved to chide me at school for the same thing. She had to teach fourth, fifth, and sixth grade classes in the same room. When my class was given a reading assignment, she would be instructing another class in arithmetic. I loved to read and soon became engrossed in the adventure.

"Galen, tell me about the story I assigned." No reply. "Galen, did you hear me? Tell the class about the reading assignment." No reply. "Mr. Conrardy, are you with us today?" Sister asked as she rapped her ruler across the front of my desk.

"Huh? I didn't do it!" I said in a startled voice. Giggles from the classroom.

Sister grabbed me by my right earlobe and led me to a corner in front of the room. "Maybe standing in the corner will help you wake up and stop your daydreaming," she said in a disgusted voice.

The defining moment occurred later that summer. "Where's Galen at?" Mom asked as she set a plate of fried chicken on the table.

"I dunno," Roy answered.

"I thought you two were playing together."

"We was, but he wanted to ride his bike and I didn't want to."

"Where did you see him last?"

"Riding down by the Quonset."

"Did anybody else see him?"

"No," said Anita.

"Nope," Janice replied.

"Boys, let's go see if we can find him," Dad directed. "Dale, you check out by the barn. Roy, you look around the chicken coop. I'll check the shelterbelt and the Quonset."

Shouts of, "Galen, where are you?" and "Galen, it's time for dinner!" echoed among the farm buildings.

"Galen what are you doing? It's time for dinner," Dad said as he rounded the east side of the Quonset. "Galen!"

"Wha-huh?"

"What are you doing?"

"Uh, thinking."

"Thinking?"

"Just thinking."

"Well it's time to think about eating, OK?"

"Yeah."

"It's about time you came in for dinner young man," Mom said sternly. "Go to the sink and get those hands and your face washed, we've been waiting for you! Where did you find him?"

"He was sitting on the east end of the Quonset," Dad replied.

"What was he doing?"

"He was holding his chin in his hand and staring into space. He said he was thinking."

Years later, Mom sent me a collectible plate for my birthday. The plate depicted a young, blonde-haired boy sitting with his hand under his chin. Inscribed on the bottom of the plate was "The Thinker."

31 Teasing the Bull

In the summer of '52 Dad purchased a stud bull that was big and mean. It had fierce-looking horns and it was always pestering the cows. Dad cautioned us boys to be very careful when we were in the corral or when we were rounding up the cows for milking. He said the bull would leave us alone if we didn't tease it. Roy and I kept a wary eye out for the bull the first few weeks it was around, but we had no problems with it.

The trouble began when Mom and Dad took us to a drive-in movie south of Scott City one Sunday evening. It was an exciting movie, *A Farewell to Arms*, based on the novel by Ernest Hemingway. There was fighting, but not like the cowboys and Indians Roy and I preferred. However, we were fascinated by the bullfights. The matador, in his prissy outfit, girly shoes, and funny sideways hat, was a really good bullfighter. We loved the way he handled his red cape. Roy and I figured that he needed the little girly shoes in order to step out of the way of the charging bull so quickly. We were sorry when his final thrust of the sword ended such a magnificent animal; nonetheless, we were impressed with the matador's courage and agility.

The next day after the chores were finished Roy and I had to reenact the fighting scenes. "I'll be the matador and you be the bull," I suggested.

"No way! You be the bull!"

"I said it first."

"I don't care, I want to be the bull guy!"

"OK," I conceded, "you give me a dime to be the bull and I'll give you a nickel to be the matador."

"Huh, you're gonna pay me to be the bull guy?"

"Yep, I'll pay you to be the bull guy and you pay me to be the bull."

Roy scratched his head, "OK," he said.

After searching around we finally found an old red shirt in the machine shed that Dad was going to use for an oil rag. "Hey, this will make a good bullfighter's cape," I said. "We can grab a hold of it by the sleeves to pull it out of the way when the bull goes charging by."

Roy snatched the shirt from my hands and practiced holding it out in front of himself. He shook it up and down and then quickly stepped to the side while still holding the shirt in the same spot. "Ole'!" he cried out. "Where are we gonna do the bullfighting?"

"Let's see. Let's go in the yard. It has nice soft grass and it has a wooden fence around it."

"Yeah, just like the bullfight ring."

My attempts at being a bull on all fours proved to be feeble at best. "You're too slow," Roy complained, "and you don't have any horns."

I then put a forefinger up at each side of my head, bent at the waist, pawed the grass with my feet, and went charging at the red shirt.

"Hey, you're going too fast now! And you hooked my red shirt with your fingers on purpose!"

"No I didn't!"

"Did too!"

"Did not!"

"Did too!"

"OK, let's try something else."

"Yeah, if we only had some real horns."

"Good idea Roy! I know where some are."

"Where's that?"

"Remember that cow's skeleton about halfway down the pasture?"

"The one by that little pond?"

"That's the one. The skull has some good horns on it and we could take it and clean it up."

"When can we go get it?"

"Let's do it now."

"OK."

After we had retrieved the skull we took it into the machine shed and smoothed out the jagged edges with the bench grinder. Then we took a long screwdriver and cleaned out the dirt on the inside of the skull. After we washed out the skull with the garden hose, we resumed our bullfights. We took turns being the matador and the bull. I held the skull on top of my head, leaned forward, and attacked the red cape. Roy made a better bull because he sounded more like one.

Being the bull and holding the skull with the horns was exhausting work. "It ain't no fun being the bull," Roy said.

"You're right. What are we gonna use for the bull now?" We still hadn't gotten the bullfighter out of our system.

"Maybe we could fight our bull."

"No way! It'd throw us over the fence if it caught us with those horns!"

"What if we just teased it a little bit? We could stay on the outside of the fence and wave the red shirt at it. Then when it got mad it would run into the fence!"

"It might break through the fence and all the cattle would get out and then Dad would really get mad."

"I don't want another whipping."

"Me neither. But I think you got a good idea Roy. What if we go into the barn, open up the sliding door, and then you can wave the red shirt at it? When it comes charging at us, I'll shove the sliding door shut."

"And it'll hit its head on the door and we'll be saved!"

"Right! It'll be dizzy and walk goofy!"

"And make funny moos too!"

We were in luck. The bull was in the corral drinking water from the cow tank. I unlatched the sliding door and pulled it back. Roy began waving the red shirt. Nothing happened. I started shouting at the bull. Still nothing happened.

"It ain't paying attention to us," Roy complained.

"I know what! I'll throw a rock at it." I found a rock outside of the barn near the sliding door and heaved it in the bull's direction. It missed the bull and made a big splash in the middle of the tank. The startled bull backed up and glanced in our direction. We had its attention. "OK Roy, start waving the red shirt," I said as I jumped back into the barn.

"Look Galen! It's getting mad!"

Sure enough! The bull was pawing at the ground with its front hooves. It was shaking its head violently from side-to-side. All of a sudden, it charged straight for us with its head lowered and it was bellowing loudly.

Roy stood frozen in his tracks. His mouth dropped open and the red shirt fell to the floor. Fortunately, I shoved the sliding door shut just in the knick of time. The door trembled from the blow of the bull's head.

I rushed to a nearby window and peered out. "Hey Roy, come and look at the bull!"

"Wow! He sure is acting goofy!" The bull staggered in a slow circle shaking its head.

That evening after Dad ran the last milk cow in the barn he noticed that the sliding door had a big crack in it with splinters sticking out. "What happened to the outside of the door?" he asked.

"The bull hit it," Roy answered.

"How come?"

I stepped quickly in front of Roy. "Roy and I were looking for some sparrows in the barn to shoot with the BB gun and we heard some noise outside of the barn. We slid the door open to see what was going on and the bull came charging at us. I closed the door just in time. I think it must have seen my red baseball cap." Thank God I was wearing it!

"Well, be more careful next time."

"We will." I sure hoped this counted as a white lie.

A few weeks later Roy and I were bringing the milk cows in from the pasture to be milked. I was on the south side of the cowherd and Roy was on the north side.

"Hey, Galen! Watch out for that bull!" Roy hollered out.

I glanced to my left and noticed that the bull was snorting and looking at me. I let out a wild scream and ran with all my might towards the nearest fence. Miraculously I made it through the wire fence to the nearby safety of a haystack, even though I had lost a shoe in the process. My heart was pounding and I was gasping for air as I tried to calm down. Roy rushed to my side a few minutes later.

"You OK?" he asked.

"I-I think so."

"You got some scratches on your arms and your shirt is torn in some places. How did you run through the fence like that?"

"I ran through the fence? I must've crawled under it."

"No way! I saw you lower your head, but I never saw you stop running!"

Roy relayed the story exactly as he saw it happen that evening at the supper table. Mom was thankful that I hadn't really been cut up in the barbed wire fence. Dad was a little skeptical about Roy's story, but not enough to beckon me to the hot seat.

32 Centipede

As we finished eating early one summer morning, Dad said, "Galen, I want you and Roy to help me clean up the lumber mess behind the garage so we can drive the wheat trucks to the Quonset."

"Galen's bigger than me," Roy was quick to interject as he tried to wriggle out of helping with the assigned chore.

"You're just a big baby! You're just a big baby!" I teased.

"That's enough you two!" Dad warned. "Galen can help you lift the lumber if it gets too heavy."

"No, I won't help that big baby!" I uttered in reply.

The glare we got from Dad ended our feeble protests. We gulped down the rest of our breakfast and hurried outside to the garage.

"Hey, Galen, look! There's a cottontail!" Roy whispered excitedly as we rounded the east end of the building.

Sure enough, he was right. A cottontail sat munching on a green weed not far from where we were now crouching. "Let's see if we can get him with some rocks," I whispered back to Roy.

"OK," he replied.

We backed up a few paces out of sight from the cottontail and gathered up some small stones to throw. "OK," I said, "on the count of three we'll rush around the corner and let him have it. One, two, three!"

"Take that you wabbit!" Roy shrieked with delight as he hurled stone after stone at the fleeing cottontail.

"Yeah, take that you bad wabbit!" I echoed as I flung my stones.

"Whoa, what do you boys think you're doing?" Dad admonished as he exited through the side door of the garage.

"We're trying to get a cottontail for supper!" I exclaimed.

"Yeah!" Roy chimed in.

"I think the cottontail's too quick for you two," Dad chuckled, "besides, we got work to do." Dad had the weed cutter in his hands. With several powerful swipes from his huge arms, he chopped down the weeds near the end of the garage. "OK, let's get busy," he said as he rested the weed cutter on the side of the building.

Dad picked up a long 2 X 4 that was lying in some weeds and placed it next to the cleared area. Roy and I were instructed to follow suit by each grabbing an end of a 2 X 4 and carrying it over and placing it on top of his. After a couple trips, Roy and I had some trouble dislodging a stubborn board that was partially embedded in the dirt and weeds. We tugged and kicked and finally broke it free. As I reached down to pick up my end, Roy shouted out, "Hey, Galen, I found a big worm! Come here and see!"

Lucky for us, Dad was returning for another 2 X 4 when he observed Roy reaching down to pick up his discovered 'worm'. "Get away!" Dad cautioned as he grabbed Roy by the arm.

"Why? That's my worm! I saw him first!" Roy pleaded.

"That's not a worm," Dad said, "that's a centipede!"

"So what!" Roy squealed, trying to break free from Dad's grasp.

"It's poisonous, and it can make you very sick," Dad stated as he picked Roy up and sat him down near the garage. He then picked up the weed cutter and proceeded to chop the centipede into several pieces.

I was impressed by Dad's quick actions in saving Roy and destroying the centipede. Dad was always our hero in times of danger.

"OK, here's what I want you to do from now on," he instructed. "Each of you get at one end of the 2 X 4 and kick it free of the dirt and weeds. Then look carefully to see if there are any centipedes around before you pick it up."

I think Dad carried over several pieces of lumber while Roy and I very carefully and methodically moved one 2 X 4 over to the growing pile by the building. When we finished, Dad left to make preparations for wheat harvest and Roy and I pondered what hero games we would pursue.

That evening at supper, Dad recounted to Mom and the rest of the family our encounter with the centipede that morning. To further impress upon us the danger that contact with a centipede can cause, he told us the story of Grandpa Conrardy and his threatening experience with a centipede.

Early one spring morning several years ago when it was still very cool out, Grandpa had gone to retrieve his jacket he had left lying next to a shed the previous morning. He picked up the jacket, put it on, and began doing the routine morning chores. Suddenly, he felt something crawling down the back of his neck and along his shoulder. Grandpa jerked his jacket off, ripped off his shirt, and flicked the centipede off his shoulder. "They had to take Grandpa to the doctor to have him treated because centipedes have poison in their front legs," Dad said as he concluded his story. Roy and I sat there wide-eyed, frozen to our seats as we listened. I had nightmares for a week about a centipede crawling up my pant leg.

It seems that we eventually have to confront our worst fears – fears that are magnified when we are young. And at the top of my list were centipedes.

A few years later Dad dropped me off in a field to run the tractor. I was elated! It was finally my turn to help with the fieldwork. We had a Case 500 tractor that had a large lever that was pushed forward to put into gear, and pulled backward to stop it. Tractors had no protective cabs at that time.

I was pulling a one-way that turned the soil over, which helped kill the weeds. I had almost made a complete rotation of the field when I felt something creeping down my pant leg. I froze. "Oh my God! It's a centipede!" I screamed. I jerked the lever back, stopping the tractor. I jumped to the ground from the rear of the tractor and began kicking and hollering.

"Oh God! Help me! I don't want to die!" I cried out. I kicked so frantically with my right leg that I actually kicked off my laced-up work shoe. I could still feel the centipede inching down my pant leg. "Oh my God! Oh my God! Somebody help me!" I pleaded in desperation. With fear gripping every fiber of my being, I began beating furiously on my leg with both fists. I was exhausted. I couldn't speak. I could still feel the centipede crawling down my leg.

Finally, as a last ditch effort, I unbuttoned my jeans and dropped them to my ankles. I stepped out of them and stood shaking uncontrollably as I glanced at my leg. I could see several red indentations on my thigh. As tears welled in my eyes, I began stomping on the pant legs of my jeans in a blind rage. Several seconds later, still sobbing, I tried shaking the mutilated centipede out of my jeans.

To my surprise, my rosary beads tumbled to the ground. After recovering from my shock, I realized that it was my rosary beads that had slid down my pant leg. I soon discovered a hole in my right jean pocket. And the rosary beads matched the imprints on my leg perfectly.

I knew I needed to thank the Lord for the passing of this would-be crisis, but under the circumstances, it was hard. It would be several years before I would carry a rosary in my pocket again.

33 Where Do Babies Come From?

Roy and I hated drying dishes. It was an assigned task we couldn't avoid until our two sisters, Anita and Jan, were old enough to take over. Older brother Dale had graduated to helping Dad with the outside chores, so we were stuck. Mom was the washer, we were the dryers. Boy, she was fast! It was all that Roy and I could do to keep up with her. We had discovered over a period of time that if we got Mom talking, she would slow down and we would actually be waiting on her. Sometimes we would ask her silly, frivolous questions. How are old are you? Do you like cowboy and Indian movies? Which of us kids do you like best? Other times we were more introspective. Where does the rain come from? Why doesn't the sun shine all day? Can you see God?

One question, though, seemed to bother her. Her face would become flush, and she would beat around the bush for an acceptable reply. I was the one who usually brought up the question, even though Roy always added his, "Me, too!" litany to my inquiry. The question was, "Where do babies come from?"

Mom gave us a stern look and furiously scrubbed a pan as she pondered her response. "Well," she said, "as I've told you hundreds of times before, the stork delivers babies."

"What's a stork?" Roy demanded.

"It's a big bird, stupid!" I interjected.

"Now Galen," Mom cautioned, "be nice."

"Is it as big as a chicken?" he added.

"Much bigger," Mom explained, "and, it can fly."

"How does it carry the baby?" I inquired.

"It has a big white towel, like the one you boys are drying dishes with, only it is probably twice as big. Then the two ends are tied together like this." She demonstrated by grabbing one of our towels.

"How could it carry the baby?" Roy asked.

Once again, Mom demonstrated for us by holding one arm out and draping the tied towel over her hand. "My arm is like the long beak of the stork," she said. Then she put the towel around her neck and pretended to have a broken arm to add emphasis to her demonstration. That made sense to me eventually, but Roy seemed puzzled by it.

"Who puts the baby in the towel for the stork?" Roy demanded.

"The angels do," Mom said gently.

"Well, where do they get the baby from?" he continued, struggling to make sense of it all.

"From God, of course," she answered. Any time that God was the answer, we didn't pursue that line of questioning. We didn't want to go to hell forever.

"Where does the stork take the baby to?" I asked.

"Well, to the hospital," Mom replied.

"How comes they don't take the baby to its mommy and daddy?" Roy questioned.

"Because the doctors at the hospital want to make sure that it's OK first," she stated. That seemed like a logical explanation to us.

I guess this question was always in the back of our minds, and our classmates' at school, too. When I was in the fifth grade and Roy was in the fourth grade, we thought we had finally arrived at the solution to this burning question. One day during lunch, Roy and I were sharing our desserts with our cousin Billy. He had split a huge cinnamon roll in two for us. Billy and I were plotting a way to convince our mothers to let one of us stay overnight with the other, when Roy interjected with, "Yeah, I know where babies come from."

"Oh, yeah!" Billy responded, "I bet you don't."

"I bet you don't either," I said, trying to act important.

"I bet you don't either, Galen" Billy quipped, grinning at me. I hated it when Billy one-upped me in the front of my little brother. Billy would always win the knowledge battle. He had older brothers who were in high school, the Navy, and some were married. And they knew almost everything there was to know. I was always impressed by them.

"Well, where do they come from, then?" I managed to mutter.

"Yeah!" Roy demanded.

"They come from your mommy's tummy," he enlightened us.

"No!" I gasped in amazement.

"You're lying! You're lying!" Roy hissed.

"No, I'm not! You stupid morons!" Billy warned.

"If you're so smart, how do they get it out of their tummies," I challenged.

"I'll show you on the chalkboard," he said confidently. Billy found a piece of a chalk and began to draw. He drew a stick figure on the board with a large, round tummy and a smaller head with long, stringy hair. "Now when the baby is ready to come out," he demonstrated with the chalk, "the mommy pees it out."

"No! That's crazy!" I yelled.

"I'm telling Sister," Roy cried out.

"No, don't do that," Billy said worriedly, "here, I'll give you a penny."

"OK," Roy said excitedly.

"Swear?" Billy wanted to be sure.

"Cross my heart, and hope to die," Roy promised.

"But," I said, reeling from this outrageous information, "how comes the baby don't drown in the toilet water?"

"Yeah," Roy interrupted, "what happens if you flush it down the toilet?"

"You dumb morons," Billy said in an exasperated voice, "they do it at the hospital."

"Really?" I asked. "How do they do it at the hospital?"

"Yeah?" Roy echoed.

"Well, you see, at the hospital the doctor stands under the floor where the toilet stool is and when they flush the toilet he catches it." Made sense to us.

When we went into the hallway to put our lunch pails away, Roy was ecstatic. "I can't wait to tell Dale and the girls when we get home," he beamed.

"Naw, we don't want to do that," I cautioned.

"How comes?" he asked.

"I tell you what," I said, a light suddenly flashing in mind, "if you give me that penny Billy gave you, then we'll keep it a secret. Just you and me."

"OK," he smiled as he fished for the penny in his bib overalls.

34 No Homework

There were several fears to contend with when we were growing up on the farm. First was the fear of getting caught doing something we knew we were not supposed to be doing. The second fear obviously goes hand-in-hand with the first one. If we were caught, then we usually had to wait until Dad came in from his fieldwork in the evening to receive our spankings. The third fear was what we imagined from hearing a scary or frightening story from the adults – like the one about poisonous centipedes. The fourth fear we had to encounter was the most humiliating because it usually occurred in front of our peers or siblings.

I was a big shot when I was in the sixth grade. Brother Roy was in the fifth grade and sister Annie was in the fourth grade. We were all situated in the big classroom of the two-room schoolhouse located north of the Catholic Church. Brother Dale was in the opposite classroom for seventh and eighth graders. My important status was about to abruptly change.

Spring had finally arrived, the weather was nice, and noon was approaching. Sister Alberta had just finished demonstrating the proper procedure for working some math problems on the board for us sixth graders. After assigning several problems to do in our textbooks for homework, she remembered to collect our homework assignments from the day before. My buddy, Bobby Kreutzer, had the honor of collecting the homework papers that day. Unfortunately for me, Sister was thumbing through the papers before she dismissed us for lunch. "Galen, I don't see your homework paper. Did you forget to turn it in?"

My face turned beet red as I stammered, "Y-y-yes, I did."

"Did you forget to bring it with you this morning?" she inquired.

"Yeah, that's right," I said with a sigh of relief.

"Yes, what do you want, Roy?" Sister asked as she acknowledged his waving arm. I was doomed.

"I don't think he did it Sister. He was playing with our neighbor Duane."

"How do you know he didn't do his homework Roy?"

"Because they wouldn't let me play with them."

"Is this true, Galen?" Sister demanded.

"I guess so," I murmured.

"Come here! Right now!"

"Yes," I said, as I slowly slid out of my desk chair and began the long trek to the front of the classroom. My classmates were snickering as I inched by them.

"Come with me young man," Sister yelled as she grabbed me by the left earlobe. "You can do your math homework at the Sisters' house while I eat my lunch!" I could hear cousin Billy poking fun at me as Sister yanked me toward the door.

The Sisters' house was just a block south of the school across from the Church. Sister finally let go of my earlobe about halfway to the house, however, she kept scolding me about the importance of being prompt and warning me about the punishment I was sure to incur from my parents when they found out. While I was fighting back my tears I was thinking about the whipping I was going to give Roy when I had a chance. Plus, he was going to have to give me a quarter to make me quit.

We entered the house through the back door by the kitchen.

Sister Mary was baking something. It really smelled good.

"Who is your new friend?" Sister Mary asked kindly.

"This is Galen Conrardy, Sister. He forgot to do his math homework," Sister Alberta said in a disgusted voice.

Sister Mary winked at me as Sister Alberta ushered me into the dinning room. "Have a seat, Galen, I'll get you some jar lids to measure."

Our homework assignment in math had not been that difficult. We were supposed to measure the diameter of four different sizes of jar lids. It only took me about ten minutes to complete the task.

"OK, Galen, you may go back to school now. Next time remember to do your homework!" Sister warned.

"Yes," I said as I looked away from her stare with tears still welled up in my eyes.

"Here Galen," Sister Mary whispered as I tried to sneak by her in the kitchen. She handed me three large chocolate chip cookies fresh from the oven. The aroma was amazing.

"Th-thanks," was I all could muster as she placed them in my hand.

I hurried out the back door and wiped the tears from my eyes with the back of my hand. Now I was going to have to face the taunts and jeers of my classmates, especially my cousin Billy and my friend Bobby. I wanted to clobber Roy but I knew they would defend him while they teased me. I would catch him at home sometime. I decided to hide out by the Knights of Columbus building, which was just across the street from the school, until it was time for afternoon classes to begin.

When I saw Sister Alberta coming down the alley towards school, I hurried across the road and into the schoolhouse. "Here comes the big baby who didn't do his homework," cousin Billy shouted out as I headed down the hallway to the classroom.

"Yeah," Bobby chimed in.

Tears were starting to well up in my eyes again when Billy

asked, “What ya got in your hands?”

“Some cookies I got from the Sisters’ kitchen,” I replied trying to hide my eyes.

“Can I have one?” Billy demanded.

“Me too!” Bobby said.

“O-OK,” I said as I handed them each a cookie.

“Wow! These are good and warm,” Billy exclaimed. “You say you got them from the Sisters’ kitchen?”

“Yes, when I was leaving the house.”

“Hey guys!” Billy proclaimed as he put his arm around me, “Galen stole some cookies for us!”

I was the center of attention at afternoon recess that day. On the way home from school Roy gloated to Mom about my ordeal at school. “Is he going to get a whipping from Dad?” Roy grinned.

“Roy told on Galen,” Annie interjected, “and Galen had tears in his eyes.”

“No, it sounds like Sister Alberta took care of things,” Mom said as I glared at Roy. “Now Galen, don’t you do anything to Roy,” she admonished. I didn’t have to, Billy and Bobby thought I was a brave guy. I was going to bask in my glory for a few days.

35 Big Game Hunting

Roy and I were always fascinated with cowboy and Indian movies. We also had favorite comic books that featured our heroes. Roy preferred Roy Rogers (obviously), while I liked Gene Autry. We both liked the Lone Ranger and Tonto. The Indians' mastery of their bows and arrows fascinated us. We tried several times to emulate them by attempting to create our own bows and arrows. A lath stick found in the back of the machine shed became our first bow. I successfully split it in two by using one of Dad's wood chisels. Roy and I each had our own bows, now we needed to come up with some string for them. Mom's ball of heavy white string that she kept by her sewing machine seemed the perfect solution to our problem. While Roy pretended to beg Mom for some cookies from the cookie jar, I snatched three arm lengths of white string from the ball. I hurriedly stuffed the string in my bib overalls and went whistling out through the kitchen. Brother Roy took his cue and followed me outside. We headed for the machine shed as fast as we could go.

"Do mine first," Roy pleaded.

"I gotta notch the ends first so we can tie the string to it," I replied.

"OK," he said.

We used Dad's bench grinder to notch a groove on both ends of the sticks. I took the string, cut it in two, and tied a double knot at each end of the stick. We had to painstakingly undo and retie our strings several times. It was either too loose or too tight. We were finally content with our prized bows. The lath stick had some give to it when we pulled back on it so we figured they were perfect. Now the search was on for a nice thin twig that we could use for an arrow. After several minutes of searching, we found a couple of twigs that we were satisfied with. Once again, the bench grinder came in handy as we ground off the rough spots. We were finally ready to become fierce warriors! We had gone from pretending to reality.

"We need some targets," I suggested.

"Where are we gonna get 'em," Roy enthused.

"Let's hide our bows so the girls won't find them, then we'll go into the house and get us some paper and draw our own targets." We hid our bows behind some oil barrels by the shed and headed for the house. Mom was surprised when we asked for some paper to draw on and some crayons. We quickly drew a couple of bull's-eyes on our paper and returned to get our bows. We grabbed a handful of nails from the nail box in the shed, got our bows and headed for the haystack behind the Quonset. Roy held the bows as I tacked our targets to the hay bales with the nails.

"Are you ready?" I said excitedly.

"Yeah," Roy added, "I get to shoot first!"

"You got any money?" I asked.

"No, I gave you my last nickel yesterday," he frowned.

"Well, what do you have?"

"Nothin' I guess."

"How's about I get your dessert at dinner?" The aroma of Mom's cherry pies baking when we were in the house drawing our targets suddenly dominated my senses.

"How comes?" Roy wanted to know.

"So you can be the first to shoot your target."

"I don't know. I love dessert."

"You can steal Jan's," I offered.

"Well, OK," he said as he drew aim on the target. The arrow landed at his feet. "That didn't work very good," he muttered in dismay.

"Here, let me show you how to do it," I interjected as I drew the string back on my bow. Same results. The arrow lay at my feet. Roy tried again and gained a few more feet this time. Encouraged by his effort I drew the string back as far as I could. Snap! My bow broke into two shattered pieces, held together by a piece of string.

"Stupid bow," I said as I flung it at the haystack.

"Yeah, stupid bow," Roy mimicked, as he threw his in the general direction of mine.

The light came on a few days later when I spotted Mom using some rubber bands to secure a lid to a box that had some of her stuff in it. "Hey, Roy," let's make us some bows and arrows again."

"They don't work," he said, minding his own business.

"But I know how to make them work now."

"Don't neither!"

"Do too! Come with me and I'll show you." I quickly grabbed a handful of rubber bands out of the utility drawer in the kitchen and headed outside. Roy shuffled slowly behind me. We found another lath stick and split it in two again. After some experimenting we discovered that four of the larger rubber bands looped together were about the right length. We hurried out to the haystack and were surprised to find that our targets were still somewhat intact. Roy picked up our arrows from where we left them before. With trembling hands we drew back our arrows and left them fly! Our arrows hit the bales of hay and fell harmlessly to the ground. We tried several more shots, but we didn't have much success hitting our targets. The arrows didn't seem to have much zip when we shot them. We eventually gave up trying.

Several days later Roy and I were watching Dad change the

inner tube in a flat tire on the pickup. When he finished this task, he tossed the ruined inner tube at us and said we could have it to play with. We were elated! We took turns trying to throw it around a post in the yard. Tiring of this, we chased each other around with it in a game of tag. Then we proceeded to get into a tug-of-war match with it. I was impressed with how much this rubber tube would stretch. Bingo!

"Hey, Roy, I got a great idea!" I shouted.

"No, you're not getting my dime," he said defensively.

"I don't want your money! I know how we can make a great bow and arrow!" I jerked the rubber inner tube from his hands and headed for the machine shed. We found Dad's tin snips on the workbench and cut two, long rubber strips from the inner tube approximately two inches in width. We tried the split lath strips again for the bows, but they just buckled under the strength of the rubber tubing. "I got it," I exclaimed as I grabbed a saw from the wall of the shed. "Follow me!" I ordered.

"Where we goin'?" Roy said as he tried to keep pace with me.

"To find us some bows," I replied as I headed for the shelterbelt located south of the chicken coop.

Dad and some of our neighbors had planted some young trees in rows to form a shelterbelt a few years before. I cut a couple of branches that were the right length. They were pliable and fit our hands just right. We returned to the machine shed, and after smoothing some of the rough spots on the bench grinder, we attached the rubber strips to them. We were impressed! They really looked liked bows this time. We fashioned a couple of twigs into arrows again and headed for the haystack. Our arrows bounced off the bales of hay with a good deal of force. No matter how many times we tried, we couldn't get the arrows to stick. "Let's go back and sharpen them on the grinder," I suggested.

While I was busy trying to sharpen the end of a twig on the grinder, Roy absent-mindedly picked up one of Dad's welding rods that was lying on the bench and tried shooting it with his bow. "Hey, did you see that thing go!" he said in amazement.

"What?" I said, distracted from my task.

"This welding rod makes a great arrow. Look," he said, as he shot another one.

"Wow! That's great!" I grabbed a handful of welding rods and began to sharpen the tips on them. When I finished we returned to the haystack. The arrows penetrated halfway into the bales of hay from fifteen to twenty feet away. We had competitions to see who could hit the same bale of hay the most.

"This is boring," Roy said as he lost the contest again.

"I know," I said, getting hit with another brainy idea, "let's hunt deer!"

"There ain't no deer around here, stupid."

"But we can pretend."

"How you gonna do that," he demanded to know.

"I got it! The chickens will be our deer! Let's go Tonto!" I yelled at him.

We slowly stalked our prey. Several "deer" were feeding near the shelterbelt. I hid behind a tree with brother Roy shadowing me. "Here comes a couple of them," I whispered as I held a finger to my lips for silence. I raised up my bow, fitted a welding rod in the rubber strip, and pulled it back. I let the arrow loose and it hit the "deer" in the back with a dull thud. The "deer" slumped to the ground and began squawking loudly. "Hurry up!" I admonished my brother, "shoot your arrow into it, too."

"OK," he said as he rushed forward. Four arrows later our "deer" lay silently at our feet. "What are we going to do with it?" Roy asked, a worried look etched on his face.

"I know, we'll dump it in the alfalfa patch." Forty acres of alfalfa grew on the south side of the shelterbelt. Our mighty war party managed to bag at least six more "deer" before it was time for dinner.

Years later, at Mom and Dad's fortieth wedding anniversary I presented a "Do you remember…" account of some of the humorous incidents that occurred on the farm when we young. This happened to be one of the incidents that I briefly recounted for them. "I wondered where those dead chickens came from when I was mowing the alfalfa hay," Dad said in exasperation, glaring at Roy and me. Some things are better left unsaid.

36 Run Over by the Jeep

"You're up early this morning Galen," Mom said as she fried bacon and eggs for our breakfast. "Did you forget to do your homework or study for a test?"

"No, we're having races today!" I exclaimed excitedly.

"What races?"

"To see who gets to go to Leoti for the track meet."

"When's that?"

"Next week."

"Who gets to go?"

"That's why we're having races today, to see who gets to go."

"I see, and how many get to go?"

"The first three boys and the first three girls."

"Well, good luck!" Mom smiled at me.

Yes, this was the Big Day! Sister Alberta was going to line up all the boys at afternoon recess to determine who would represent the fourth, fifth, and sixth grade students at Leoti. There were eleven boys competing for three spots. The girls then had a race to see who would represent them.

Cousin Billy had first place nailed down – no one could catch him. Bobby Kreutzer would probably get one of the spots, and I definitely wanted one. Traditionally the three representatives for the boys came from the sixth grade class – if they had enough boys in the class. Younger brother Roy, who was in the fifth grade, was the fastest boy in his class. But he didn't dare challenge me!

During morning recess, each class huddled together in their chosen areas of the playground to map out their strategy and to make practice runs. There were four boys in our sixth grade class: me, Billy, Bobby Kreutzer, and Bobby Brown. Sure enough, in our practice runs it was Billy followed by Bobby K. and then me. Bobby Brown was so small his little legs just spun in one spot.

During lunch, after we had teased the fourth and fifth graders about our impending victories, we settled down to talk about the big Wichita County Track Meet. We wondered how many boys would be there from the other schools, if there would be many cute girls there, and what kind of prizes we'd get for winning the races.

Finally, Sister Gertie rang the bell for afternoon recess. The big event was about to happen! "OK, you boys line up here by the fence," Sister instructed. "You will run to the tree at the other end of the playground. Wait until I walk down by the tree. When I blow my whistle, you can start. Remember, no cheating! I will pick the three winners. Any questions?"

As Sister made her way to the tree, Billy lined up in the middle of the starting line and Bobby K. and I flanked him on either side. The rest of the boys then filled in along the starting line. I was nervous. My mouth was dry. My palms were sweating.

Sister raised her hand to get our attention. She slowly put the whistle to her lips and the loud shrill penetrated our beings. We were off!

I ran as hard as I could, pumping my arms and gasping for breath. Billy was easily four or five paces ahead of me and I could make out Bobby K. a couple of paces in front of me to my right. After I passed Sister Gertie standing by the tree I slowed down and joined Bobby K. who was congratulating Billy.

Sister Gertie blew her whistle to get our attention. We quickly gathered around her to get the results of the race. "The first place winner is Billy Conrardy." We all clapped as he strutted his stuff. "Second place goes to Bobby Kreutzer." More clapping ensued. "However, it seems we have a tie for third place."

"What?" I exclaimed, shocked by this revelation.

"Yes, we have a tie," Sister continued, "between Galen Conrardy and his brother Roy."

"Are you sure?" I blurted out.

"Yes," she said, "we're going to have a runoff. Galen, you and Roy go back to the starting line and wait for me to blow my whistle."

"You better not let the sixth grade class down," Billy sneered as I turned and headed for the starting line.

"Yeah," Bobby K. snickered.

My face was turning beet red and my heart was pounding as I jogged to the other end of the playground. Roy followed close behind me.

As we lined up, I glanced at my brother and he gave me one of his ear-to-ear grins. I was in such a state of shock I failed to either bribe him or warn him of the consequences should he win. Sister raised her hand and we raised ours in return to indicate that we were ready. We sprang forward at the sound of her whistle.

Roy and I were neck and neck as we huffed and puffed our way to the finish line. I closed my eyes and I strained with every fiber of my being to win third place.

Sister's announcement of the third place winner who would get to go to Leoti was interrupted by cheers of, "Way to go Roy! You beat your brother! Yea for Roy and the fifth grade!"

I was stunned. My little brother had beaten me by a full step.

"Roy gets to go with us to Leoti!" Billy taunted as he put his arm around Roy's shoulders.

"Yeah, you big loser," Bobby K. said as he joined Billy and Roy.

I was embarrassed. I was devastated. I was totally humiliated.

I wanted to hide. Forever. Anywhere.

Anita informed Mom on the way home from school of my defeat at the hands of my brother. Roy didn't say anything as I sat sobbing in the back seat. Mom tried to console me with, "You'll do better next time Galen." But there wouldn't be a next time for me.

"What's the matter with Galen?" Dad asked as we sat down for supper. I was totally withdrawn in my self-pity.

"Galen got…" Anita began.

"Stop it," Mom interjected. She then relayed the events of the afternoon race to Dad.

"You know, I've been thinking these past couple of years that you seem to walk funny at times," Dad said. "I've got to go to Scott City Saturday on business, so I think I'll take you along to see the chiropractor and have him check your legs out."

Dad's suspicions were correct. Dr. Young, the chiropractor, said his examination revealed that my left leg was approximately one-half inch longer than my right leg. He said people are sometimes born with one leg longer than the other one. However, he pointed out that mine was caused by my left hip being out of alignment with my right hip. "I think that a fall or a blow to the hip may have caused it," he said. He felt that a series of treatments could straighten the problem out.

On the way home Dad questioned me about any falls I may have taken from a tree, building, or haystack. Nothing came to my mind that would be major enough to cause such a traumatic shift in my hips.

That night at the supper table Dad recounted what the chiropractor had said, including the part about a fall or blow to my hips causing my walking and running problems.

"Maybe it was when he got run over by the jeep," Roy offered.

"What!?" Dad and Mom said in unison.

"Yeah, Dale ran over him," Roy stated.

"No I didn't!" Dale said.

"Did too!"

"Did not!"

"Whoa!" Dad interrupted. "Dale ran over Galen?"

"It was an accident," I said.

Three years earlier Mom had sent us three boys to fetch Dad for the noon meal. He was working in the field a mile south of the farm.

Dale was driving, Roy was in the middle, and I was sitting by the passenger door. We were in the jeep, which had a manual transmission. Mom had instructed Dale to drive in compound gear (the lowest gear range), so we were probably moving along at about five miles per hour.

"Someone's coming behind us with a tractor and drill," Dale said as he glanced out at the side mirror.

"Really?" I asked. "I wonder who it is?"

"I can't tell for sure. The mirror is too dirty."

"I'll see," I said as I opened the door to take a peek. Not being able to see anything, I leaned out further. My hand slipped from the door handle and I boomeranged under the slow-moving jeep. The right rear tire bumped over my hips and I rolled into the ditch. Dale stopped the jeep and he and Roy came running back to check on my condition.

"Are you dead yet?" Roy asked.

"Yeah, are you OK?" Dale pleaded.

"I, I think so." I said. I slowly rolled over on my side. "My hips kinda hurt though."

"Here, help me get him out of the ditch, Roy." It didn't hurt too badly if I walked slowly with short steps.

"We better hurry before the tractor catches up to us," Dale said as he and Roy helped me into the jeep. We continued on our way to get Dad for dinner. "Remember, let's don't say a thing to Mom and Dad about this, OK?"

I didn't eat much for dinner that day and I took an

uncharacteristically long nap. When I got up late that afternoon I felt fine except for the soreness in my hips, and I still had to take short steps.

The expected spankings didn't occur. Instead, Dad and Mom pleaded with us to always report any accidents to them as soon as possible. Our health and safety was paramount, they instructed us.

37 The Slingshot

"Galen and Roy, after we finish eating breakfast I want you two to round up those stray calves in the pasture and lock them up in the corral," Dad said.

"Why can't Dale do it?" Roy protested.

"Because he's helping Bill haul hay bales."

"Make the girls do it," he whined.

"That's enough young man! You and Galen do as you're told!"

"But..."

"Do you want a whipping from Dad?" I whispered.

"No, but..."

"Well, shut up then!"

When breakfast was finished, Roy and I headed for the pasture. "Hey, wait a minute Brutus! Let's take our weapons in case we see some snakes."

"Yeah," Roy said, "good idea. I get the Red Ryder BB gun."

"OK, I'll use that neat slingshot we made yesterday."

Roy and I had fashioned a really great slingshot. The trees in our shelterbelt had been growing by leaps and bounds, so we cut off a forked branch from one of the trees that seemed perfectly Y-shaped. Using the bench grinder, we smoothed the ends of the Y branch and then notched a circular groove approximately one inch from the end of each branch of the Y. Next, we cut two rubber strips from an old inner tube for the slings. They were twelve inches long and half an inch wide. We then looped each strip around the groove at each end of the fork and secured them with a piece of baling wire. The final step was to cut a two-by-three-inch rectangular piece of leather from the tongue of an old shoe that we had found. We carefully measured and cut a slit near each end of the leather piece. Our slingshot was complete when we inserted the end of each rubber strip through a slit in the leather piece.

The initial testing of our slingshot was a great success. It would shoot a small rock an inch in diameter one hundred feet pretty accurately.

While Roy filled the magazine of the BB gun with BB's, I found several small rocks for the slingshot. I filled both of my bib overall pockets with them. "Are you ready to go?" I asked.

"Yeah, let's go kill some snakes," Roy answered.

"Well, I really hope we don't see any." I knew that the BB gun would only agitate them if we shot at them. And I had no idea how powerful the slingshot was. We opened up the corral gate south of the barn and headed down the pasture. The six calves that had managed to get out of the corral were all at the far end of the pasture, a half-mile away. Roy and I both shot at a couple of meadowlarks on the way down, but we only managed to spook them into flight.

It didn't take long to get the calves headed back in the direction of the corral. A few shots from Roy's BB gun and my slingshot did the trick. In fact, they had all gone in the open gate of the corral before Roy and I were halfway back, except for one. One of the bigger calves, approximately 700 pounds, had headed north along the outside of the corral to the corner of the pasture fence. I instructed Roy to stand guard about fifty feet east of the open gate so that he could help herd the calf into the corral after I rounded it up from the corner and headed it in his direction.

I grabbed a nice, smooth, round rock from my left pocket and fitted it in the leather patch of my slingshot. I held it in the ready position between my thumb and forefinger. As I neared the calf, it backed up into the corner of the fence, lowered its head, and just stared at me. I frantically waved my arms and tried to make it move. It just stood there, eyeing me. Panic began to set in. What to do?

The calf took a couple deliberate steps in my direction. I raised the slingshot, took aim, and released the rock. There was a dull thud. The calf staggered a step or two and fell over. My shot had hit the calf right in the middle of the forehead. I approached the calf cautiously from the side. It just lay there, eyes staring straight ahead.

"You killed it! You killed it!" Roy panted as he ran to my side.

"I didn't do it on purpose! It was going to attack me!"

"Boy, Dad's gonna whip your butt good! You won't be able to sit down for a week, maybe a month!"

"Yeah, I know. That's what I'm afraid of. Come on, let's get out of here. Go close the corral gate and meet me at our secret hideout."

"OK, but Dad's sure gonna be mad at you!"

Roy met me in our little cave that we had constructed out of straw bales near the haystack. "I don't know what we're going to do. We gotta get rid of that calf or hide it somewhere."

"I know," Roy said, "we could burn it! Remember when cousin Billy burned the hair off their milk cows?"

"Hey, yeah! Nah, that won't work."

"How comes?"

"Because it just burned the fuzzy winter hair off the cow and it didn't hurt it."

"Yeah, that's right, I remember now. But it was sure funny when he lit the cow's hair under its belly and it whooshed up its side like a blanket being pulled up. Maybe if we poured some gasoline on it first."

"That might work! No, it would make too much smoke and they'd probably smell it, too. Hey, we could get a couple of shovels and dig a hole and bury it."

"Boy, we'll have to dig a deep hole. You think if we prayed, Jesus would help us?"

"I wish. I don't think He helps you when you do something wrong. Come on, let's go get those shovels."

Roy and I went to the shed and grabbed two spade shovels and headed dejectedly for the corner of the pasture where the calf lay. "What are we gonna do if we get caught?" Roy asked as we neared the fence.

"I dunno," I replied.

"Hey, where's that calf?"

"Right over there you stupid…" The calf had disappeared.

"What happened to it?"

"It was lying right over there."

"That's what I thought."

"Maybe someone stole it!"

"I don't think so, we would have heard them."

"Maybe Dad already put it in the pickup and is waiting to catch us. I'm gonna tell him you did it. I saw you!"

"Don't you da— Hey look! The calf is down by the corral gate!"

"It's a miracle!"

"I know. You sneak down into the corral and open up the gate. I'll walk down and scare it in when you get it opened."

"OK."

When Roy opened the gate, the calf bolted in without much prodding. We picked up the shovels and headed back for the shed. "I guess Dad won't have to whip you now."

"I know. Thanks for praying! Would you like to have that nickel back that I won from you yesterday?" Atonement for one's sins came at a price.

38 Rats in the Barn

A few years after our new barn had been built we discovered a major problem – RATS! The northwest corner of the barn had a dirt floor. A single sliding door opened to an outside pen. We bottle-fed the newborn calves and we used this as a holding pen for them. Bales of straw were scattered on the dirt floor for the baby calves to recline on. The back portion of this area had a wooden enclosure, much like a huge closet, where we stored the ground grain for the milk cows.

The rats had tunneled under the outside concrete foundation, or had simply made their way through the sliding door when it was open. Then they burrowed and nested under the wooden grain bin. Roy was the first to notice these pests when he was getting a bucket of grain to feed to the milk cows. "Hey, there's a big mouse back here," he hollered out.

We rushed back to the grain bin, but didn't see any. Dad noticed several holes near the outside of the grain bin's wooden floor. "I don't think we have a mice problem," he said, "I think we probably have a rat problem. Why don't you boys try to get some of them after the chores are finished? You can use that little .22 rifle you got for Christmas. Use the birdshot ammo. There's a box on the shelf in the machine shed."

We were elated to get to use the gun and help get rid of a

problem at the same time. It would be just Roy and me because it was the opening day of pheasant season, the second weekend in November, and Dale was going on his first hunt with Dad and his hunting party. Dad had purchased a single shot .410 shotgun for Dale to use.

After we had gathered eggs and deposited them in the basement to be cleaned and sorted, Roy and I went to the gun cabinet and withdrew the .22 rifle. We boys were really fond of this little rifle because the last six inches of the wooden stock underneath the barrel folded down for a handgrip. Roy found the birdshot shells on the shelf in the machine shed where Dad said they would be. Birdshot was the correct choice to use; it wasn't as lethal as a .22 rifle shell, but it packed enough of a wallop to kill rodents.

When we entered the barn, we walked quietly behind the stanchion trough where we fed the cows. We then crouched down behind the cement trough trying to spot some rats running around in the holding pen. I loaded a dozen shells in the rifle's magazine and injected a shell into the chamber. The gun was a single shot, bolt-action model.

"Hey, there's one Galen!"

"Where?"

"Over there by the corner of the grain bin!"

"Oh, I see it!" I took careful aim and squeezed the trigger. Thud! The bullet found its mark. The dead rat lay kicking on the dirt floor.

"Good shot! Hey, I see some more running around! It's my turn! It's my turn!"

"OK." I ejected the spent shell casing and loaded another one into the chamber. I handed the gun slowly to Roy with the barrel pointing away from us. "Be careful. Get a good aim."

"Oh, there goes another one now," Roy said. The rat paused momentarily at the rat hole. Roy squeezed the trigger, another thud, and the rat lay by the hole.

"Good shot Roy!"

"Yeah, I did good, didn't I?"

Roy handed the rifle back to me and I loaded another shell into the chamber. We waited patiently for another fifteen minutes, but no more rats showed. "Let's try again before noon," I said. I unloaded the shell from the chamber of the gun and we scooped the rats up in a shovel and took them out in the pasture to bury.

"OK, let's go play baseball," Roy said.

We went back shortly before noon and waited for ten minutes, but no more rats appeared. "Let's go eat, " I told Roy.

The hunting party Dad invited to dinner consisted of the Ford dealer – Mr. Elmers from Scott City – and three of his friends from other parts of the state. One of them was a professor from Kansas University in Lawrence. As we were eating Mom's scrumptious chicken dinner, Dad asked Roy and me how our rat extermination project was going.

"We got two!" Roy blurted out. "Galen got one and I got one!"

"Sounds good. You didn't see very many, huh?"

"I think there's quite a few. They just got scared when we started shooting," I said.

"And we saw a couple of white ones too," Roy added.

"Really?" the professor from K.U. asked.

"We sure did," I replied.

"Albino rats are really valuable for lab research," the professor said, "and they are hard to come by."

"Well, you can have them all," Dad laughed, "you just have to catch them first."

"Really? I'd love to come in a couple of weeks and catch all that we can."

"How about two weeks from today?" Dad offered.

"That would be great! I'll bring my assistant along and we'll bring plenty of cages for them. We'll be here by 9 a.m."

"We'll look forward to seeing you then," Dad said, shaking the professor's hand. "Boys, we'll wait to shoot the rest of the rats until the professor gets his white rats."

Sure enough, two weeks later the professor and his assistant showed up at about 8:30 a.m. Dad had them park their school van near the barn. They unloaded several small cages and some nets and took them into the barn. When they finished unloading their gear they put on rubberized clothing, boots, and gloves. Dad was wearing a pair of knee-high rubber irrigation boots and they gave him a pair of rubber gloves to wear. The rubber gear was a precaution against rat bites, the professor claimed.

The procedure for catching the rats was a simple one. Dad attached a garden hose to the faucet in the milk room and unrolled the hose into the holding pen. While he ran water from the high-pressure nozzle into one of the rat holes, the professor and his assistant stood slightly to the front and on either side of the rat hole with their closely knitted nets ready to go. If a rat came struggling out of the water-filled hole that was not an albino, they let it go. The only place for them to go was in another hole or outside of the barn.

Dad had made preparations to get rid of the ordinary rats. He reasoned that all of the rat holes would eventually be full of water so the only other avenue of escape was through the sliding door on the north side of the barn. Before he started drowning the rats out, he positioned Dale, Roy, and me on the outside of the barn to the left of the open door. This way we would be shooting parallel to the barn into an open area. He filled the magazines of the two rifles with birdshot and told us to alternate shots unless more than one rat came out at the same time. Dale got to use the lever-action Marlin .22 and Roy and I took turns using the small .22 that we had used before.

We boys had a little side bet going on. If Dale shot more rats than Roy and I did, we owed him a quarter. If we got more than he did, then he owed us a quarter. Ironically, this helped ensure that

Dad's strategy worked perfectly.

The water-soaked rats ran around the pen in a confused state before opting for the safety outside. They scrambled up the ledge to the doorframe, then dropped approximately six inches to the ground on the outside. Once they hit the ground, they paused momentarily to get their bearings. Then we plugged them. Dale had the first shot and his aim was true. Usually the rats plopped on the ground one at a time, but occasionally two of them made it at the same time. When this happened, Dale directed us on which rat to shoot, while he shot the other one. Because he had the first shot and the advantage of having the lever-action rifle, he shot three more rats than Roy and I did. The final tally was Dale ten, Roy and me, seven. Dad was proud of us because not a single rat escaped, even though it cost Roy and me a quarter.

The professor and his assistant were very pleased because they had bagged eight albino rats. The University would probably use these white rats for breeding purposes in order to help keep a supply for the research lab, the professor stated. They offered to compensate Dad not only for the albino rats, but also for his time and effort in helping them. Dad refused payment, stating that if it was for a good cause, then it was worth it. Besides, he added, it helped get rid of our rodent problem.

They also suggested pouring concrete on the dirt floor to ensure that the rats wouldn't return. A few months later the floor was solid concrete.

"What do you think they did with them white rats in their research lab?" Roy asked one morning when we were putting down clean straw on the concrete floor for the newborn calves.

"I dunno for sure," I replied, "but I bet they sell their tails to the witches."

39 Girls

Girls were a nuisance. They were always interrupting us, wanting to play in our games. And if we let them, they usually quit because we "weren't playing fair." They were spies for their mothers and the nuns and they loved tattling on us. Seventy percent of our whippings were directly attributable to them. The only thing they were good for was to tease and taunt. We loved to make them cry and beg for mercy. Our favorite chorus line was, "Cry baby! Cry baby! Who you gonna go bawling to now?" Sometimes our mothers and the nuns even got tired of their constant whining.

For some strange reason our attitudes towards these unacceptable creatures began to change when we entered the seventh grade. The most noticeable change was that they had physically matured over the summer months. They were much taller and there were bumps showing on their chests – some more pronounced than others, especially on the eighth grade girls. Cousin Billy said that they had tits like milk cows had. We argued that it couldn't be so because cows had four tits. He remained adamant in his assertion.

Not only did the girls look strange, but they also began acting strange. They now giggled and blushed when they glanced in our direction, or pointed at us and withdrew into a whispered huddle. Our initial assessment was that they were crazy.

Our perception slowly began to change when we caught Billy talking to one of the eighth grade girls during recess. When we cornered him later and accused him of messing around with a girl, he dared us to make something of it. We decided that it must be OK if Billy was doing it. Bobby Kreutzer and I eventually followed suit. Yvonne Betlock became the object of my affection. A typical conversation with her went like this:

"Hi, Galen."

"Hi."

"What ya doing?"

"Nothing."

"I like your Guy Lombardo shirt."

"Yeah."

"What did you bring for lunch?"

"A sandwich."

"Well, I guess we'd better get to class."

"Yeah."

We became more daring in the next step of our relationships – writing and passing notes. There were basically three ways to pass notes: directly (person-to-person), by use of a drop zone (such as her desk or lunchbox), or by courier (having one of your friends deliver the note for you). You used a courier if you were cool. Our notes were actually written in sentence form, although the content value was questionable.

Dear Yvonne,
I like my Guy Lombardo shirt too.
You have a nice dress.
Did you see Billy and Mary holding hands?
Bobby said he did. I don't believe it.
Do you?
Galen

The defining moment in our initial relationships occurred when we openly declared our fidelity to one girl. This was not a verbal outburst, but rather a visual one. It began by boldly printing on our arms, hands, or fingers who the apple of our eye was. Billy + Mary, Galen + Yvonne, Bobby + Jean. We were proud to flash these proclamations to our peers, and especially to our girlfriends. These visual displays soon found their way onto our writing tablets and books. And if you wanted to be daring or tease someone, you would print it in chalk on a corner of the chalkboard. The ultimate expression of endearment was to carve it on the desktop or on a tree with a jackknife. The thing was, you never wanted to get caught in the act of carving. If you were confronted because your name or initials had been carved, you could always feign innocence or blame someone else.

The downside was getting caught by Sister passing notes or flashing our symbols of affection in class. I was the center of attention one day because I had artistically enclosed the plus sign with a heart in red ink. Billy was even jealous because he hadn't thought of it first.

Galen

Yvonne

While Sister was busy writing sentences on the board for us to diagram, I nudged Yvonne in the back. She turned in her seat and I pulled my shirtsleeve up, revealing my intricate artwork.

"Galen, what are you doing?" Sister demanded.

"Nothing, I was just rolling my sleeve down."

"Why is Yvonne watching?"

"I don't know."

"Come up here and let me see."

I reluctantly went to the front of the classroom and bared my arm for Sister. I spent the noon and afternoon recesses writing on the chalkboard, "I will not lie to Sister or write nonsense on my arm."

Roy was only too happy to reveal my misfortune to Mom and Dad at the supper table that evening. After a brief lecture on why we should never write on our arms or any other part of our bodies, Mom took me to the kitchen sink and vigorously scrubbed "Galen + Yvonne" off my arm with Lava soap. Then Dad invited me to his chair.

40 Arden

Roy and I each had our own heroes growing up on the farm. Roy's favorite cowboy was Roy Rogers, mine was Gene Autry. My favorite baseball player was Ted Williams of the Boston Red Sox, his was Roy Campanille of the Brooklyn Dodgers. We spent hours arguing whose hero was the best. He always got in a low blow with his quip, "How many heroes are you named after?" He had me there. However, my real hero was Dad. He was not only bigger than life, he was a great baseball player!

Likewise, we usually had a peer in school whom we secretly admired. Our hero was not only one of us, but he dared to defy adult authority. Roy and I had made feeble attempts to exert our independence, only to discover that the strong arm of discipline ruled.

Arden Knobbe fit the part. He was short, had reddish hair, a ruddy complexion, and a contagious ear-to-ear grin. And he was quick! He was always the first one chosen for any game where speed was paramount. Nothing seemed to faze Arden, verbally or physically. Scrapes and bruises were part of his mystique, his red badge of courage. While we whimpered and cried, depending on the severity of the inflicted pain, he reveled in it. He would bounce up from being tackled by a host of players and boldly announce, "That was fun! Let's do it again!"

Arden was a tough kid, good-natured, and he had a zest for fun! At anyone's expense. We all desired to be that tough, that resilient. The adults of the community considered Arden a "little devil." At least we all heard comments attesting to this epithet. His notoriety earned him our respect and adulation. Some of the girls pretended to be fearful in his presence, but whispered excitedly of his daring deeds in their select circles.

The crowning achievement of Arden's heroic status occurred early one spring day in school. Following lunch and noon recess, Sister Vivian had instructed the seventh graders to get out their math textbooks and pass their homework assignments to the front. She leafed through the papers as she picked them up. Halting abruptly, Sister glared at Arden and demanded to know where his homework assignment was. "I dunno," he grinned, "I think my dog ate it this morning."

"That's it! I've had enough of your lies and rudeness! Go outside and get a switch! Now! You're going to get the biggest whipping of your life young man!"

Sister Vivian was beet red and shaking when Arden slowly exited the room. Hearing our snickering brought her attention back to the class. "Now class, that's not funny. Arden's a naughty boy and he must be punished. Let's continue with the fractions on page 142."

We were busy trying to comprehend the multiplication of fractions when Sister interrupted our thought processes with, "Where's Arden? He should have been back ten minutes ago! If I have to go get…" The door slowly opened and Arden sheepishly poked his head around the corner. "Get in here right now!" Sister ordered.

Arden sauntered to the front of the classroom and stood facing Sister with his hands in his bib overalls. Sister's face began to puff out and turn red and a blood vein popped out on her forehead. Her right eye twitched as she clenched her fists. "What took you so long? And where is that switch I told you to get?"

"Right here," he said.

"I don't see anything."

Arden uncurled the fingers of his right hand revealing a small sliver of wood. "How dare you insult me young man!" Sister yelled as she backhanded him across his mouth. "Get out of here and get me a big switch because you're really going to get it now!"

Blood trickled down the corner of Arden's mouth as he shuffled towards the door. Before exiting the room, he paused, turned, and flashed a big smile for our benefit. Fortunately, Sister was trying to control her rage and failed to notice Arden's gesture of contempt. We weren't snickering now; we could feel Sister's wrath.

It took several minutes for Sister to calm down and get us back on task – it seemed like an eternity. The atmosphere of a studious classroom had just returned when Sister erupted into an emotional outburst. "Where's that kid at? He has disobeyed me for the last time! Boy is he going to get it!" Sister's arms were flailing around and her face was steaming as she stomped angrily to the door.

Just then, the door flung open, and Arden came in grunting and groaning as he dragged a railroad tie into the room. Sister Vivian stood horrified, frozen. All of a sudden, she shrieked loudly, grabbed Arden from behind, and spun him around. Uttering incomprehensible sounds, she began hitting him in the face with the palms of her hands. She would slap him from one hand to the other like a ping-pong ball, a ping-pong ball with a smiley face. Arden was saved by the recess bell.

Obviously, Arden's heroic stature among his peers grew by leaps and bounds. Many parents openly admitted they were thrilled when summer recess began a few weeks later so their kids wouldn't be around Arden.

41 Milking Cows

Vacations seemed a rare occurrence, other than an occasional holiday weekend, because the milk cows kept us on the farm. They had to be milked every morning and every evening. And when we did visit Grandpa and Grandma on a special holiday, our hired man was charged with the milking chores. Oftentimes, Dad stayed behind to help.

The milking times were pretty well set in stone – 4:30 a.m. and 5:30 p.m. As my brothers and I came of age – five years old – we were employed in the milking operation. I say 'employed' because Dad occasionally let us share a cream check he received from selling five-gallon containers of cream to a local creamery in town.

Milking the cows followed a set pattern. After opening the barn, the first task was placing a half-gallon can of grain in front of each cow's stanchion. The sliding barn doors would then be opened to admit the milk cows. Rounding up the cows in the morning was easy as they were all locked up in an adjacent corral. Our Collie dog rounded up the cows from the pasture in the evening (until it got run over by the truck), then Queenie and I would bring them in for their milking. Sometimes Roy and I walked down the pasture to get them.

We seldom had any trouble with the cows. Once the sliding doors were open, they filed in dutifully to eat their allotted portion of grain and to be relieved of their milk load. The wooden stanchions were evenly placed along the inside of the barn on both the east and west sides. A stanchion consisted of a 2 X 6 approximately six feet high and another identical 2 X 6 that pivoted back and forth on a bolt at the bottom of the stanchion. After the milk cows stuck their heads between the boards to begin feeding, the moveable 2 X 6 were locked in place with a twelve-inch block of wood on top of the stanchion.

The entire barn floor was concrete in three equal sections. Each section was three feet wider than the length of an average cow. Running the length of the floor were two gutters, four inches in depth and a foot wide. The concrete slabs all sloped slightly towards these gutters, which caught the cow manure and urine. After the cows were dismissed from their milkings, the entire concrete floor had to be hosed down with water.

When the milk cows were locked in place and they were munching on their grain, preparations began for the actual milking. Four or five of the cows always had to be hobbled to keep them from kicking. We accomplished by taking a short chain that had a U-shaped clamp attached to each end of it and securing a clamp above the knee joint of one of the hind legs, wrapping the chain around both legs, and securing the second clamp above the knee joint of the second leg.

We had two milking machines. One had dual glass cylinder containers that held five gallons of milk each. The other machine had a single glass cylinder container. The dual machine could milk two cows at once, the other machine one. After the cow's udder and tits were thoroughly cleaned with soapy water, the milking apparatus was attached one tit at a time. The elongated rubber tubes had an alternating sucking motion that would extract milk from the cows. Dad and his hired man usually monitored this process.

In the meantime, Dale, Roy, and I grabbed our milk pails and each begin to milk a cow by hand. We had T-stools made out of 2

X 6's to sit on. While holding our milk pails between our knees we squeezed and pulled on the cow's tits in a downward motion with alternating hand strokes. Our contribution to the daily milking ritual was usually two cows apiece.

When Dad wasn't around we sometimes engaged in a milk fight. This took place while Dad was processing some of the milk in the milk room or when he was out of the barn. You can squirt milk from a cow's tit several feet, much like squirting water from a water gun.

Because cows were milked from the right side, you had the advantage if your brother was milking a cow somewhere to the right of you. You shoved your cow into the next cow to the left and then you did the same to the cow on the right. This gave you enough room to squirt a stream of milk over the top of the cow to your right. With a little practice, you could shower your brother with milk if he wasn't too far away.

On this particular morning, the final milk fight commenced. We boys were milking our last cows and Dad was out of the milking area. The battle started when Roy tried to squirt me from across the center floor. I was milking a cow on the west side of the barn at the far north end. Roy was milking a cow on the east side of the barn a few cows from the north end and Dale was milking a cow on the east side a few cows south of Roy's location.

"Hey, what's that?" I blurted out as droplets of milk splashed near my feet.

"Gotcha!" Roy grinned.

"Take that!" Dale joined in. Because of his angle, his squirts were landing at the back of the cow's legs.

"No fair," I complained, "I can't get you back!" I could squirt the cow to the left of Roy, but that didn't do any good. By leaning in towards the cow I was milking I was able to avoid most of the milk that was squirted my way.

It was about this time that Roy decided to shift his target from me to Dale. Once again, because of his strategic position, he had the definite advantage. His first couple of shots over the top of the cows were short, so he kept adjusting the angle of the cow's tit and the pressure of his squeeze. Finally, a few drops of milk fell on Dale's head and shoulders. "Dang it, Roy!" Dale shouted out.

"It's your turn!" Roy laughed.

Dale tried getting back at Roy by squirting under his cow. His attempts were futile as the milk was about a cow's width short from reaching Roy's legs. However, he was able to avoid most of the milk shower by scooting in close to his cow as I had done with mine.

Regardless of who had the advantage, most of our milk fights usually ended with taunts and threats of who was going to get whom the next time. Having exhausted the milk supply in one of the tits, Roy switched to another one. Dale took this momentary lag as a cue that the milk fight was over. As he glanced up his face was showered with milk. "Boy, you're going to get it!" Dale sputtered as he tried wiping the milk from his eyes.

"Galen told me to do it," Roy said in self-defense.

"Like heck he did," Dale admonished. He then threw his milk stool down and grabbed his pail of milk. He rushed over to Roy and dumped the pail of milk over the top of Roy's head. "Take that you little devil!" he yelled.

"I'll kill you!" Roy screamed. He caught his breath and took after Dale. Roy was the fastest of us three, so he was right behind Dale as they entered the milk room.

"Whoa, what's going on here," Dad demanded as he grabbed Roy and Dale by an arm.

"Dale threw his pail of milk on me," Roy squealed.

"He started it Dad," Dale whined.

"I don't care who started it," Dad said, "it's a sin to waste milk. I don't ever want to see you boys do that again!"

A few protested swats from the rubber strap ensured the warning stayed with us.

42 Touching the Communion Chalice

Farm chores (doing dishes, gathering eggs, milking cows, feeding the pigs, and tending the garden) were assigned – unsolicited responsibilities. Serving as an altar boy at church was a coveted responsibility we boys all sought. If you were a boy, Catholic, and attended the Immaculate Heart of Mary Church, then you qualified for altar boy service. The only restriction was age – you had to be a fourth grader.

There were several reasons that made being an altar boy so special. First, you were out of Mom and Dad's parental jurisdiction. Second, you got to say all of that Latin stuff with the priest, like "mea culpa, mea culpa, mea maxima culpa." And, most importantly, you got to wear the long black cassock with the white tunic top. Grandpa and Grandma were impressed when they visited, and so were the girls!

Becoming a fourth grader didn't automatically ensure that we became altar boys. We had to undergo intense training, at least we thought so, before we had the privilege of actually serving at a Mass. Our initial session with Sister Gertie – she was in charge of altar boy training – was a guided tour of the sacristy and the altar area. Sister showed us how to dress, where Father's vestments were, and where the sacred items used in the Mass service were located. She made a special note at that time to inform us *Not To*

Dare touch the sacred chalice. To do so was to invite the wrath of God! We might be struck by lightning or something. We new recruits were almost speechless. We were going to be joining an elite group!

The most difficult part of the training was mastering the Latin terminology. Sister Gertie had printed in very large type our Latin responses that we would say during the course of the Mass. Not only that, she had them broken down by syllables and marked phonetically. Repetition of these Latin phrases and sentences was the key to how quickly we earned our places in the rotation of Mass servers. Having an older brother to practice with at home always helped.

These practice sessions always took place immediately after school in Sister Gertie's classroom. She usually spent thirty minutes every Monday, Wednesday, and Friday going over the Latin terminology. Tuesdays and Thursdays were spent practicing and rehearsing the order of the Mass in the church. Once Sister Gertie deemed us competent, we were given the privilege of serving at our first Mass. It usually took a month to reach this first step.

Younger brother Roy also became a server when he was a fourth grader. He achieved altar boy status in the same time as most of us had done before him. Once he became a server, he was usually assigned altar boy duty with me. At most Masses, two altar boys assisted the priest. On very special occasions, several altar boys might be required.

One summer afternoon Roy and I had to go to church to practice for an upcoming wedding. After dropping us off, Mom went grocery shopping at the little store that was located just northwest of the church. Father gave Roy and me some instruction while we waited for the wedding party to show up. After a quick walk-through with the wedding participants, Father departed with the wedding couple for their final briefing at the rectory. Roy and I saw to it that everything was put away in its proper place. While we were in the sacristy area, we stood and marveled at the gold chalice. It was particularly stunning that afternoon with the sunrays that filtered in through the stained glass windows reflecting off it.

"Boy, I wish I had that!" Roy uttered in amazement.

"So do I," I replied.

"I betcha can't touch it!" he challenged.

"I don't want to be struck by lightning," I quipped back at him.

"Me neither!" he said, his eyes getting large.

Deep in the recesses of my mind, a recollection started to emerge. Cousin Billy had claimed that his older brother Leland had once touched this sacred chalice and lived to tell about it.

Roy still had a shiny silver dollar that he had received from his godfather for his birthday a few weeks previous that I highly coveted. "I was just thinking," I said matter-of-factly, "that I just might touch that gold chalice."

"Really?" Roy cried out in amazement.

"Really. I just might do it," I retorted somewhat courageously.

"I'll tell Mom and Dad," he warned, "you'll be hit by lightning from God!"

"Yeah, you're probably right," I said, "nobody would dare do such a thing!" The seed had been planted.

"Oh yeah, well, I dare you to touch it!" he declared.

"Well, I'm not going to touch it for nothing," I said encouragingly.

"I'll betcha five marbles that you can't do it!"

"I've got more marbles than you do already," I admonished. "However, I just might do it for your silver dollar."

"No way! That's mine!"

"OK," I replied, "let's go find Mom at the grocery store."

"Wait," he implored, "what do I get if you get struck by lightning?"

I thought a moment as I scratched my head. "I know. If I get struck by lightning, then you'll get the silver dollar!"

"Hey, yeah, then it'll be mine," he said excitedly. "I dare you! I dare you!" he taunted.

"I don't know," I said weakly, the thought of getting struck by lightning looming ever larger.

"I double dare you!"

Nobody backs down from a double dare. As his jeering eyes watched, I closed my eyes, shuddered, and slowly inched my trembling fingers over the white linen cloth towards the chalice. Eternity flashed before my eyes. Suddenly I felt something cold, metallic.

"You're gonna be killed!" Roy screamed as he ran from the sacristy.

I couldn't move. My fingertips were still frozen to the base of the chalice. I slowly opened one eyelid, then the other. I was still alive! I was still alive! Finally, as the shock subsided, I withdrew my hand and stood there in amazement.

After calming down, I realized that I better find my brother Roy, and quickly. As I raced out of the church, I dreaded facing Mom – I knew that Roy was pouring out his soul to her. I waited for a passing car and scooted across the street to the grocery store. Sobbing noises brought me to a halt next to our Ford car. I glanced in the rear window and noticed Roy curled up in a ball, crying uncontrollably. With a sigh of relief, I opened the rear door. "Hey, Roy, it's OK, I'm alive!"

"Are you really?" he said, peeking at me.

"Yes, I am," I said, giving him a hug.

I shared that shiny silver dollar with him at the five-and-ten store in Scott City.

43 Playing Baseball

We boys grew up playing baseball. It was the only game in town, so to speak. We played it during the summer months at home and during recess at school. When we were old enough to play Little League baseball, Dad signed us up with the Wolves team in Leoti. Our sponsor was Green Butane who delivered fuel to the farm.

Leoti was the county seat of Wichita County and was located six miles west of Marienthal where we went to church and school. The summer before we moved to a farm in eastern Colorado, Dale was selected as an outfielder from our team to play on the Leoti All Star team. They began their quest to make it to the Little League World Series, which was held in Joplin, Missouri, by beating the Colorado All Stars at Leoti. Next up for the All Stars was a trip to Burlington where they beat the eastern Kansas champions. Their road to the Little League World Series ended in a regional tournament in Oklahoma.

Our love for baseball was fueled by Dad's passion for the game. He pitched and played first base and in the outfield for the town team in Marienthal. Dad could throw hard, he was a great hitter, and he had speed on the base paths.

Mom was Dad's biggest fan. She really got involved in the game. When the home team got a base hit, or Dad struck out an opposing batter, she'd be yelling her head off and honking the horn on the family sedan. If things were going in favor of the other team, then the umpire would take the brunt of her verbal assaults. Sometimes Roy and I would excuse ourselves to go to the outhouse so we could sneak to the other side of the ball field.

During the middle of the Dirty Thirties, Dad played baseball for a Van Johnson team in Dodge City. He gained a reputation for his prowess on the mound and for his keen eye at the plate. So much so, that the Detroit Tigers and the Philadelphia A's wanted to sign him to a contract. But, because of the tough times on the farm, Grandpa Conrardy felt that his presence was needed there.

Dad's fondest memories from this time were when he got to pitch against Satchel Paige and Lefty Grove. Lefty Grove was retired at the time and pitching for a traveling team. Dad's team won handily. However, he lost a close contest, 4 – 2, to Satchel Paige and the Kansas City Monarchs. After the game when Dad was shaking Satchel's hand, Satchel quipped, "If you was just a colored boy, we'd take you with us."

One of my most memorable recollections of Dad's ball-playing days was when the Marienthal team was playing a crew of railroad workers who were temporarily stationed in town. The Missouri Pacific Railroad was resurfacing several miles of tracks at the time.

Dad was pitching for the home team. By the end of the second inning, Dad's team was leading 12 – 0. In the top of the third inning, the railroaders sent up a tall, lanky kid to the plate. The very first pitch, a high fastball, nailed the railroader right in the middle of his forehead. He dropped his bat and crumpled to the ground. Dad had trouble controlling his high fastball at times. He rushed to the plate, obvious concern etched on his brow. One of the players on the bench rushed out with a jug of water. He splashed some water on the railroader's face. The umpire and the catcher then grabbed him by the arms and helped him to his feet. They kept their grip on him, as his legs were still quite wobbly. Dad placed his hand gently on the railroader's shoulder and apologized to him for his wild throw. The railroader, while trying to focus his gaze on Dad, replied, "Hits me in the head and breaks both ankles!"

To encourage our interest in the game, Dad put up a backstop north of the house for us. He cut up some old telephone poles and placed four or five deep in the ground. Some extra chicken wire fencing was then tacked to these poles. It was great! Now we didn't have to waste time chasing passed balls.

If Dale, Roy, and I were playing, one of us would bat, one would field, and one would pitch. After a designated number of swings and hits, we would rotate positions. However, quite often it was just Roy and me playing because Dale would be helping Dad with the farm work.

Roy and I emulated our favorite teams. His was the Brooklyn Dodgers; mine was the Boston Red Sox. Whenever Dale played, his favorite team was the New York Yankees, which was also Dad's favorite. Roy liked the Brooklyn Dodgers because of their catcher, Roy Campanella. I liked the Boston Red Sox because of their great hitter, Ted Williams, who was left-handed. Any time a game involving one of our teams was broadcast over the airwaves, we would huddle anxiously around a radio.

The battle was on when Roy's Dodgers and my Red Sox met on our playing field. We greatly modified the rules because it was just the two of us.

Whoever happened to be carrying the bat when we reached the ball field would toss it gently, grip end of the bat up, in the air. The other player would grab the bat from the air with one hand. Then we would take turns placing one hand above the other. The player with the last hand left holding the grip end of the bat was the home team.

Our rules were the same for strikeouts and walks. A foul ball judged catchable was an out and any grounders or pop-ups that didn't make it out of the infield were also outs. Short fly balls in the outfield were also automatic outs. And there were no stolen bases or double plays.

Ground balls out of the infield were singles, hard line drives were doubles, and fly balls hit over the road in the outfield were homeruns. A line drive hit down the third base line or the first base line were triples if they reached the road ditch.

The pitcher determined balls, strikes, and outs. The batter was responsible for calling the hits and the advancement of the runners on base.

Our games, which always went the full nine innings, sometimes lasted several days. Chores, meals, and the weather often delayed the completion of our games. Of course, there were those times we couldn't play because we didn't have any equipment. It was confiscated when we were caught playing ball instead of finishing a chore. But when we were finally able to resume our game, we always knew what the score was, what inning it was, and who was batting or pitching.

A typical game always began with a challenge. "Hey, Roy, I bet my Red Sox can beat your Dodgers today," I said.

"Can't neither," he replied, accepting the bet.

"OK, let's get our stuff and play."

"I'll find the ball and bat, you get the gloves."

"OK, let's hurry before the girls see us and want to play."

We gathered our gear and hurried to the field. "Go ahead and toss the bat up," I directed.

"Catch," he said.

I grabbed the bat in the middle and we took turns placing one hand above the other. "You're home team," Roy announced as I grabbed the end of the bat.

"Who's pitching for the Dodgers?" I asked.

"Johnny Podres. Who you pitching?"

"Mel Parnell." We were both going with our aces. "Good luck."

"Yeah, you too."

I strolled to our makeshift mound. "Are you ready?" I yelled. We provided our own play-by-play.

"Yeah. The first batter up for the Dodgers is the second baseman, Jackie Robinson."

"Mel Parnell winds up and throws his first pitch, a fastball."

"Jackie lets that go by."

"It's a called strike, strike one. Looking for his sign, Mel nods his head and hurls his next pitch, a curveball."

"Jackie swings and hits the ball. It looks like it made it by the third baseman into the outfield."

"Yeah, it barely made it out of the infield," I said.

"It's a single for Jackie. Next batter up is Pee Wee Reese, the shortstop. Runner on first, nobody out."

Pee Wee struck out and Gil Hodges, first baseman, walked. Duke Snider popped up for the second out. Roy Campanella, the catcher, hit a double, driving in a run. Dick Williams, right fielder, was hit by a wild pitch and the bases were loaded. Mel Parnell then issued a bases loaded walk to the left fielder, Cookie Lavagetta. With the score now 2 – 0 in favor of the Dodgers, Bobby Morgan, third baseman, grounded out to retire the side.

When my Red Sox came to bat in the bottom of the first inning, the same lengthy play-by-play ensued. Johnny Podres, the Dodgers' ace, walked Milt Bollig, shortstop, and Bill Consolo, second baseman. With runners on first and second, Jackie Jensen, right fielder, popped up to the infield for the first out. Ted Williams, left fielder, then hit a single to right field to load the bases. Dom Dimaggio, center fielder, recorded the second out by flying out to center field. With two outs, George Kell, third baseman, and Sammy White, catcher, each hit a single to drive in a run apiece. Faye Thronberry, first baseman, grounded out to end the inning. At the end of the first inning, the score was tied 2 – 2.

We reveled in announcing our own play-by-play. The pitching and hitting almost seemed like afterthoughts. Regardless of the outcome of our games, we always left the field complimenting each other on how well our teams had played. No nickels or dimes changed hands and we never got mad at each other.

44 Halloween

Our initial impression of Halloween was twofold; our parents complained about it, and it was apparently very scary if you were a bad kid. A recent whipping we had received made us worry about the scary part.

Mom and Dad's complaints seemed justified until we came of the age to participate in the pranks. When we went to church one Sunday morning following Halloween, Dad had to maneuver the car through an obstacle course of farm machinery and building materials that local teenagers had dragged out onto Marienthal's main street – two blocks long. Of course, all the neighbors joined in the chorus of complaints, too. Father also mentioned in his sermon that the destruction of property was definitely a sin. All eyes turned disapprovingly in the direction of those teenagers who were present at Mass. They shifted nervously in their pews and kept their eyes cast down. Roy and I got caught up in the thrill of being chased by the local town cops after we moved to Stratton – whose main street was three blocks in length. Apparently, littering the main streets of small towns in the 1950's was a farming community thing.

The scary part involved cousin Leland, one of Billy's older brothers. On Halloween night 1953, two of Leland's uncles on his mother's side showed up at their farmhouse in black hoods. They burst into the house unannounced, grabbed Leland, dragged him outside, and tied him to a tree with a log chain. He was left there all alone, frightened and screaming for several minutes. Mom always said that incident had an effect on Leland's later behavior. Well, Roy and I certainly didn't want the Diller brothers to tie us to our big cottonwood tree. Besides, I wasn't too fond of the dark.

We did enjoy seeing who could carve the meanest-looking pumpkin. I usually waited until Roy was about finished with his pumpkin so I could figure out what to do to make my pumpkin spookier. We then polled our sisters to see who won. I even had to give the girls each a nickel once to make sure they picked my pumpkin.

The Halloween costume parties at school were fun, too. Roy and I went one year as Roy Rogers and Gene Autry, and the next year we went as the Lone Ranger and Tonto. Although we only won a prize once, third place, we really looked forward to the treats. There were all kinds of homemade candy, popcorn balls, and cupcakes to choose from. And no one protested when we went for seconds.

Roy and I got to go trick-or-treating for the first time in 1954. We went with my classmate and friend, Bobby Kreutzer, who lived in Marienthal. Bobby had his ghost costume on, and Roy and I were attired in our usual cowboy outfits. "Ready to go?" Bobby asked as he grabbed a flashlight from the kitchen table.

"Yeah," I said somewhat apprehensively.

"Me too," Roy added.

We were nervous, but we were eager to fill our huge candy sacks with goodies. And we figured Bobby knew what he was doing. Our first stop was at a retired couple's home. Bobby rang the doorbell and Roy and I stood silently behind him. A nice white-haired lady answered the door. "Trick-or-treat," Bobby announced.

"Oh my, we have three scary creatures at our door," she said. She turned and called out to her husband, "John, bring the candy jar here and save me from these spooky characters."

John arrived with the candy jar and gave us the evil eye. "Humph, I think we'd better see the tricks before we give them the treats, don't you Ma?"

"Yes, that would be a good idea," she grinned.

There was a long pause. Finally the old gentleman said, "Well?"

Bobby started flapping his arms and yelling out, "Boo! Boo! Boo!"

"What's the matter with your two sidekicks Casper, cat got their tongues?"

I stood awe-struck and frozen in my tracks. Roy finally uttered a weak, "Boo, boo," behind me.

"I guess that'll do," the old man chuckled. He then placed a handful of candy in each of our sacks.

As we were walking to the next house, Bobby chewed us out for not helping him with the trick performance. "I said boo two times," Roy said.

"But you guys are cowboys, pull your guns out and tell them to stick 'em up."

"OK," we said in unison.

After we left our next trick-or-treat call, Bobby told us that we did a little better. "Next time though, tell *them* to stick 'em up, don't do it to each other."

We were working our way slowly across town from east to west. The first place we came to on the west side of town was a small one-story house. "This is where old Tom lives," Bobby stated. "Let's see if he'll give us a treat." Old Tom was a bachelor, a real recluse. No one really knew what he did for a living.

Bobby gave three solid raps on the door. We waited for a few seconds and then Bobby repeated the knocking. Once again, no response. Bobby told us to holler 'trick-or-treat' real loud while he tried knocking on the door again. It was deadly silent.

"Maybe he's dead," Roy cautioned.

"Let's peek in the kitchen window," Bobby said. We could see a little old man huddled over the kitchen table staring at something. "We'll stop by on our way back to my house and try again," Bobby promised.

Our sacks were getting heavy from all the loot as we headed back across town. There was still a light on in old Tom's house. "Are we going to try it again?" I queried.

"Just as well," Bobby replied.

"Yeah, just as well," Roy mimicked.

We followed the same procedure as before with the same results. We peeked in the window again and old Tom was still in the same position. "Well, I guess he gets the trick," Bobby warned.

"What are we going to do?" I asked.

"Yeah, what?" Roy chimed in.

Bobby looked around the yard using his flashlight. "Look over there!"

"Where?" I asked.

"At that pile of coal."

"What about it?"

"Let's pile it on his doorstep next to his door. Then he won't be able to get out!"

"Good idea," I enthused. We spent the next twenty minutes carrying several armloads of coal to the cement doorstep. There was a four-foot high pile of coal blocking the door when we finished.

"That'll teach him not to give us a treat," Bobby said.

I had a dream that night that old Tom had starved to death because he couldn't get out of his house because of the trick we had pulled on him.

The next morning when we went to church in Marienthal, I noticed that the coal was back in its original pile. We didn't take into account that his door opened to the inside. I was relieved.

45 Polio

It was scary. People were talking about it. It was an epidemic that was sweeping across the country. The adults were comparing it to the spinal meningitis that had ravaged their communities when they were young. Polio was an infectious virus that left its victims temporarily or permanently paralyzed. Severe cases had to be placed in the Iron Lung. The Iron Lung was a body-length, stainless steel cylindrical tube. This contraption aided the patient in breathing.

Much as the Israelites in Biblical times had prayed for the Angel of Death to pass by overhead, so did the families and communities of western Kansas fervently pray for polio to bypass them. However, polio would strike, and close to home.

Cousin Melvin Conrardy, one of Billy's older brothers, was hit hard by polio. Melvin was an aspiring sixteen-year-old athlete who loved baseball and life. He was one of Dad's favorite nephews. Dad said he would have been a great catcher. Melvin was permanently paralyzed from the waist down, with partial paralysis of the arms and hands.

Besides Melvin, Uncle Anthony and Aunt Rose's second oldest child, Delbert, also contracted the dreaded virus. Delbert was serving in the Navy at San Diego, California, at the time.

Fortunately, Delbert's bout with polio was temporary, but it caused the Navy to give him a medical discharge.

"Galen, do you think we'll get polio?" Roy asked.

"I sure hope not, but I'm scared. Melvin and Delbert got it."

"I hope Billy and Sammy don't get it."

"Me too."

"What is polio anyway?"

"Well, I'm not sure, but I think it's this thing that floats in the air. Mom said that some people are bowlnerable to it – whatever that means."

"Are we bowlnerable Galen?"

"I don't exactly know."

"Can't we do nothing about it?"

"Mom says we should pray a lot."

"How comes?"

"So Jesus will make it go away."

"How comes He didn't make it go away for Melvin and Delbert?"

"I dunno. I guess because they were bowlnerable."

"Can't He do nothing about bowlnerable?"

"I guess the devil must have something to do with bowlnerable."

"What do you mean?"

"Well, maybe if you do something really bad, then the devil can make you bowlnerable."

"Wow! I wonder what Melvin and Delbert did that was so bad?"

"Maybe Melvin said ten naughty words one day."

"Boy, we better not say no more naughty words!"

"Yeah, we better not let Jesus or Mom and Dad hear us."

"What about Delbert? What did he do to make him bowlnerable?"

"Let's see. He's in the Navy, and Billy said that you had to swim if you were in the Navy. Maybe Delbert didn't clean the swimming pool when he was done swimming."

"Yeah, but we don't have no swimming pool!"

"Yes, but we do have a bathtub now. So I guess we better start cleaning it up after we take a bath."

"But we don't swim in the tub."

"We try to. Besides, Mom says that you and I always leave a dirty ring around it."

"I'll help you clean it from now on so we won't be bowlnerable, OK?"

"If you give me a dime, you can clean it."

"How's that going to help?"

"Because you get to pay not to be bowlnerable."

"OK."

Thank God for Dr. Jonas Salk and the polio vaccine. We began our vaccinations after we moved to Stratton, Colorado, in 1955.

46 Leaving Home

We three boys were returning home from Church with Dad one Friday evening during the autumn of 1954 when he made a surprising announcement. “Boys, we’re going to have to sell the farm here. We’re going to move to a farm at Stratton, Colorado, next spring when you’re out of school.”

I was stunned, Roy was looking at his baseball cards, and Dale asked, “Why?”

“Because we couldn’t get the financing to buy our landlord’s land here, and they want to sell.”

“Is it like our farm here?” Dale continued.

“Not quite. It’s hilly and the soil is sandy. But, we are going to build a new house there.”

“That’s great!” Dale said excitedly.

I couldn’t believe my ears! We were going to move? How could that be? We couldn’t leave home! Home was home. There could never be another home. Jesus must be punishing me. I wondered what I had forgotten to say in the confessional a few moments ago.

I was so fearful that I became very superstitious. My magic life-saving number was three. Whatever I would do had to be in a sequence of three. If I turned a doorknob, it had to be three times before I opened the door. When I said my morning and evening prayers, I had to say each prayer three times. If I answered a question in class, it had to be three times. "I think the answer is twenty-six, let me think – twenty-six, yes it is twenty-six." This went on for four or five years before I was finally able to work it out of my system.

A couple months before we moved to Colorado, we had to move to Marienthal temporarily and rent a house to live in. The sales contract on the farm stipulated that we be off the premises by a certain date. The only house available to us was a little three-bedroom sod house on the east side of town. It was cramped, but we managed to make do. Living in town was a thrill; we were big shots now. With the addition of seven family members, the population of Marienthal swelled to seventy-two. It was a different feeling being 'city folk'.

After we moved to town, we still had to make daily trips to the farm after school to feed the chickens and gather the eggs. Our neighbors who bought our chickens weren't able to pick them up until two weeks after we moved to town. Dad had been in Stratton during that time getting things settled for our upcoming move there. He returned early on a Saturday morning, and that afternoon he took us boys with him to gather the eggs for the last time and load up some personal items we still had at the farm. Dad pulled up by the shed in our pickup. He instructed Roy and me to gather the eggs in the egg pails we had brought along, and he told Dale to help him load up some tools and equipment that were still in the shed.

It didn't take Roy and me long to complete our task. We gathered up two pails of eggs and then scattered some grain for the hens for the last time. When we finished, we noticed that Dad and Dale were still busy in the shed, so we decided to play tag by throwing chickens at each other. We each grabbed a chicken by its wing tips and slowly rocked the chicken back towards our chests. Then we flipped it in the direction of our intended target. Feathers flew everywhere and the chickens were in a squawking frenzy. Dad entered the chicken coop and barely avoided being hit by a flying chicken. "What in tarnation is going on in here?"

As luck would have it, I was caught in the act of flipping a chicken at Roy. "Galen's throwing chickens at me!" Roy cried.

"So was he…"

"Drop that chicken and come here!" Dad interrupted.

I panicked and headed for the open door. As I was running past Dad, he pivoted and kicked at me in disgust. The toe of his boot caught my right thumb as I swung my arm back. The pain shot up my arm into my shoulder like lightning bolts. I burst into tears. I couldn't catch my breath, it hurt so much.

Dad grabbed me from behind. "What's the matter Galen? Did I kick your hand?" He looked at my hand. My thumb was bent backwards and was swelling rapidly. "Oh my God!" he said. Dad made me look the other way and with one quick motion, he yanked my thumb back into place.

He put his arm around me and carefully led me to the pickup. I was still crying uncontrollably. "Just calm down now. You're going to be OK." He took a roll of electrical tape from the glove compartment and taped my thumb gently to the side of my hand for support and protection.

On the way back to town all Dad could muster was, "That's what happens when you don't do as you're told." I think that the strap would have been less painful.

Uncle Bill arrived from Stratton with his truck to help us move. We loaded all our furniture and belongings on his Chevy truck and Dad's Ford truck that afternoon. The next morning we said goodbye to Uncle Anthony, Aunt Rose, and their boys. Our close neighbors, the Wilkens, were also on hand to see us off.

The journey to Stratton was approximately 150 miles and it took us four hours to get there. Dale rode with Uncle Bill in his truck, the girls rode with Mom in the car, and Roy and I rode with Dad in the Ford truck. As we crossed the state line into Colorado on

Highway 24 near Kanorado, Dad said, “Well, here we are boys. This is Colorado.”

In 1955, eastern Colorado was in the midst of a mini-dust bowl. The fence lines and ditches were full of dirt and several dust eddies could be seen whirling on the barren fields. “I want to go home,” I whispered. “I want to go home. I want to go home.”

Breinigsville, PA USA
22 September 2010

245921BV00004B/34/P